Expanded Second Edition

Know You Have Eternal Life.

Get Deliverance

From Curses and Traumas!

1 John 5:13 Mark 16:17

RUTH S. OLSON

Copyright © 2023 Ruth Solveig Olson
All rights reserved.
Contact me: givingyeshua.com

**Know You Have Eternal Life.
Get Deliverance
From Curses and Traumas!**

ISBN: 978-1-945423-61-1

Unless otherwise indicated, all Scripture quotations are taken from the Holy Bible: King James Version (KJV) (1611; public domain in US).

Scripture quotations marked (CJB) are taken from Complete Jewish Bible, Copyright © 1998 by David H. Stern. All rights reserved.

Scripture quotations marked (NKJV) are taken from the Holy Bible: New King James Version®. Copyright © 1982 by Thomas Nelson. Used by permission. All rights reserved.

Scripture quotations marked (TLV) are taken from Tree of Life Version Translation of the Bible. Copyright © 2015 by The Messianic Jewish Family Bible Society.

> Copyright notice. All materials contained within this book are protected by United States copyright law and may not be reproduced, distributed, transmitted, displayed, published, or broadcast without the prior, express written permission of the author. You may not alter or remove any copyright or other notice from any copies of this content. The sole exception to this notice is, you may copy the questionnaire, providing reference is given to this book and author. For questions, please contact the author through the website above.

Contents

Dedication	4
Acknowledgments	5
Prologue	7
Instructions Regarding Deliverances in This Book	11
1 The Name of the Savior, Yeshua	15
2 My Story	17
3 The Spanish Inquisition and It's Effect Today	27
4 Remitting Sins	31
5 Know You Have Eternal Life and Questionnaire	35
6 The Biblical Feasts and Sabbaths are for Today	41
7 Have No Other Gods	49
8 Symbols and Emblems that Bring Curses	67
9 Teaching on Actual Deliverance	71
10 Deliverance from Curses	77
11 Deliverance from Traumas	85
12 How I Speak with People Who Need the Savior	95
13 Deliverances as I Witness	101
14 How to Keep a Person from Falling Away	105
Conclusion	107
Appendices	111
Endnotes	154
References, Contact for Authors	171
Addendum I	178
Addendum II	179
Addendum III	185
Index	189

Dedication

To Yeshua, my Savior, healer, and deliverer.

To a woman from South America who came to church with her neighbor aware of her Spanish Jew genealogy. She desperately wants deliverance from the Catholic bondages of her family. She was not sure of going to heaven when she died but hoped to go by keeping the feasts and sabbaths.

To children and adults who need deliverance and healing from the witchcraft of sexual abuse and secret orders.

Endorsements

Ruth has done a very good job with the breakdown of deliverance in her book. She will help many people with a clear vision of salvation. Great job.

Rexa Daniels' daughter, Carmella Rose

"This book by Ruth S. Olson is a masterpiece! I know that a person needs both salvation and deliverance."

Jane E. Grogan,
Board Certified Counselor/
Tele-Mental Health professional, Centennial, Colorado.

Crystal Cobb responded. In reading through some chapters of your book and taking authority to remove certain items that I knew were in my life for a very long time, Masonry and infant baptism, something has occurred. I am not driven any more. Remnants of perfectionism, being withdrawn, and silent when needing to speak, have departed. I am more relaxed, stable and steadfast, yet respecting authority without trembling has come to be a living reality. I'm more grounded and secure in my relationship with Messiah. I know he approves of me.

Crystal Cobb, Gunnison, Colorado.

Acknowledgments

My mother and father, who accepted the Savior at a youth Bible camp. My Father was a Lutheran Pastor. After retiring, Mother led a telephone prayer ministry and a weekly women's prayer meeting, and Dad conducted a weekly couples Bible study in their home.

Women in Janet Fritch's Bible study who prayed over my prayer letters, but MaryJane knew I needed prayer. Charles Doryland prayed over the prayer letters before he went to heaven.

My Messianic friend, Crystal Cobb and others who have critiqued my manuscripts. My adult children, who have prospered though they suffered with me through the difficult years of my life.

Dell F. Sanchez Ph.D., who through his books and seminars has taught us about the Spanish Jews. To messianic congregations where I learned the name, Yeshua, and experienced the biblical holidays and sabbaths. Hispanic churches in Denver, Minnesota and Mexico that I have attended. My in-laws, who provided many trips to Mexico after moving there, giving me a love for these people. The instructors of Spanish classes in churches, then in at a senior center, and my faithful classmates.

Jesus Encounter Ministries of Mark Hemans which closely resembles the ministry of Yeshua. They provided deliverance at many Online meetings during the COVID-19 lockdown, fewer now. Pastor Eloyse Badgett, Christian Living Fellowship (CLF), Be Free, Lakewood, Colorado. 1970 – 2010. In 2008

Acknowledgments

she gave a prophecy that we should spiritually battle for our country. Anna Paraseah (Raile), my deliverance counselor at CLF. Rexa Daniels (Rose), the associate pastor and counselor at CLF until 1994. Irene A. Park, author of The Witch that Switched, and seven booklets. I will speak of these as Pastor Eloyse, CLF, Anna, Rexa, and Park.

A very special thanks to my husband of 32 years, who is my skillful computer tech support.

He attends Light of the Nations church and listens to 670 am KLTT Christian radio. I have received a lot of deliverance since our marriage to improve our relationship, and I continue to pray for more deliverance for him.

Prologue

I am pleased to publish this new edition of *Know You Have Eternal Life. Get Deliverance from Curses and Traumas!* I recently published *Saber que Tienes Vida Eterna ¡Obtén Liberación de Maldiciones y Traumas! 1 Juan 5:13 Marcos 16:17.* I am updating my English version because I added over 100 pages to this Spanish book. I am including the prophecy for the Spanish Jews. I am adding more names of demons and principalities which Pastor Eloyse discerned, to use now in deliverance and spiritual warfare. Antichrist Spirits and the Illuminati, Sexual Lust Demons and more on Krodeus, the Bastard Curse. I include surveys to verify my concern that many persons in the church are not sure of going to heaven. You can locate these by viewing Addendums in the index.

"Woe to the inhabitants of the earth and the sea! For the devil has come down to you, having great wrath, because he knows that he has a short time." (Rev. 12:12b)

I want you to be saved, delivered, and reach out to others who need salvation and deliverance.

A Prophecy for the Spanish Jews

This prophecy was given to me by Yeshua and Abba Father on September 20, 2020, after a missionary couple spoke who were leaving for Costa Rica. "These are my people. I have called them by my name. They are mine. (Is. 43:1b). I see their sorrows, griefs, and heartaches; and their sins that are attacking them and their families. This book is for them, for their deliverance and healing. I have your mind. I have sent you to teach them, to comfort them, to reach out to them with love.

Prologue

Israel; they are mine. I have called them by another name. I love them more than ever for their suffering in this feast time. (September 2020, during the Fall Feasts). I have a whole lot of love for them and my land. I am sorry for the hate that most of them have for me and my people. I came to my own and they received me not, but to all who received me I gave the power to be called the sons and daughters of Yah, to all who believe on my name. (John 1:11-12). Abba.

After witnessing and singing at the viewing and funeral of a 32-year-old Hispanic woman who died from alcoholism, Yeshua told me the Jews needed to be saved. (Rom. 1:16, 9:1-4; Acts 3:22-23). Some of these Hispanics are Jewish; their ancestors came from Spain to the New World, hoping to escape the Spanish Inquisition and Catholicism that sought to destroy them.

Dr. Maurice Rawlings, a heart surgeon, saw people die on his operating table and started screaming that they were in hell. Nearly half of those he brought back from the dead had been to hell. One of them asked him to pray. Rawlings and his patient both became believers in that prayer. He wrote the book, To Hell and Back.1 (See References).

> "Wide is the gate, and broad is the way, that leadeth to destruction, and many there be which go in there at."

(Matt. 7:13b)

Apostle Paul says,

> "those who practice such things, (the works of the flesh) will not inherit the kingdom of God."

(Gal. 5:21b; 5:15-26 NKJV).

After Yeshua shed his blood, before he went to heaven, he commanded us to go with the good news, cast out demons, speak with new tongues, and heal the sick. (Matt. 28:19, Mark 16:15-20). I look for churches like this. Wherever we worship, we must worship the Father in spirit and truth. (John 4:21-24).

I am sure you know some people, even in your church, who have been baptized by sprinkling, have been in Scouting or other Freemason organizations, have been traumatized, or have suffered abuse, and they may not be sure of going to heaven.

You will be shocked to learn the satanic origin of our church holidays. Those ignorant of deliverance and spiritual warfare will not be aware of Satan's Kingdom and may be participating in it unaware. I have been receiving deliverance since 1982 and now deliver others and myself.

I received miracle deliverances from Anna in 1999 that changed my life. Why did I need deliverance? I was raised in the church and married a man whose family was in the church, but my story is worse than a soap opera.

We are to *"have no fellowship with the unfruitful works of darkness, but rather expose them."* (Eph 5:11).

I will teach about the biblical feasts and sabbaths.

Yeshua said, *"If you love me, keep my commandments."* (John 14:15 NKJV). *"Do not think that I came to destroy the Law or the Prophets. I did not come to destroy but to fulfill."* (Matt. 5:17 NKJV).

In 1996, I began witnessing on my morning walks. In April 2022, only one of the eight people I spoke with one morning was sure of going to heaven after death.

"The harvest is plentiful, but the laborers are few." (Matt. 9:37).

One must be saved, delivered, and filled with the Holy Spirit to be a witness. We are living in the end times. People must be very concerned about their spiritual condition and that of their family, neighbors, and those in their church, congregation, or synagogue.

Many believe the catching up of believers, the rapture, will be soon. (Dan. 12:1; 1 Thess. 4:13-18; Rev. 3:10). If you miss the rapture, it's because you weren't "counted worthy to escape" or because you are to be one of the 144,000 Jewish

Prologue

missionaries during the great tribulation. (Rev. 7:1-8; 14:1-6; Luke 21:36).

People who miss the rapture will go through the seven years of the great tribulation, a time of great terror over all the world. (Jer. 30:5-7; Matt. 24:21-22). Jewish people will be safe at Petra Jordan for the last half of the tribulation. (Rev. 12:6). When they are desperate, they will call for Yeshua, and he will return and save them. (Ps. 118:26; Matt. 23:37-39).

During this tribulation, the anti-Messiah's "false prophet" will deceive people, so they will worship the beast, the Anti-Messiah, and take his mark on their right hand or forehead. A Catholic man who went to heaven and returned said he was told there that some parents would take the mark to buy food for their children and then go to hell. (Rev. 13:11-17; 14:9-11; 19:20).

If you don't take the mark, you will not be able to buy or sell. If you are beheaded because of your witness for Yeshua, you will reign with him for a thousand years. (Rev. 20:4).

Tom Horn, an author with a good reputation as a prophet, dreamed about an asteroid hitting southern California on Friday, April 13, 2029, which he believes will be in the middle of the seven years of the great tribulation. (Rev. 8:11).[2] Friday the 13th is a witches' sabbath. Witchcraft has been practiced in secret, but it's now practiced openly. In a highly brazen opening ceremony to the Commonwealth Games in Birmingham, England, on July 28, 2022, many bowed down to Baal and Lucifer, portrayed as a huge bull.[3] (See, Bull on the altar of Zeus in Pergamos, The Name of the Savior, Yeshua Chapter).

Though I attended college for six years, I have no degree in theology, psychology, or medicine.

> *"But God has chosen the foolish things of the world to put to shame the wise, and God has chosen the weak things of the world to put to shame the things which are mighty."* (1 Cor. 1:27).

Instructions Regarding the Deliverances in This Book

This book is based on my experiences; while some are terrible, I started my deliverance in 1982. For any other person, I cannot guarantee the same results. I not only use the name Yeshua and keep the biblical sabbaths, but at CLF, I learned how to deliver myself and others and practice spiritual warfare. Since then, I have benefited from other deliverance ministries, deliverance and mental health conferences. I have also had mental health counsel in private and group sessions. The references I include for you in this book have been very valuable to me.

For privacy, I didn't disclose the name of any living or deceased family member or another person, except those who have already published their stories. In references, I listed contact information of several deliverance and healing ministries. However, all severe health and emotional problems should be taken to a medical professional as well as to a deliverance ministry. I and the deliverance ministries I quote are not licensed professionals.

As I prepared the manuscript for this book, I had Brother Carlos on YouTube because demons have fought this book.[4] These are strong principalities and demons. Bind the spirits of Baal and Beelzebub before you do any deliverance. (Jer. 32:35; Luke 11:14-26). (See 80-list, Appendix E). I also bind Leviathan and the trinities of Satan and Lucifer. And I bind or cast these out before interrogating demons or discerning if a song, Bible verse, or message I am getting is from Yeshua. Anna told me to pray in tongues for 15 minutes after every deliverance session. (Trinities, see Six-pointed Star, Symbols and Emblems that Bring Curses chapter).

Work with other committed believers and put on your armor according to Ephesians 6:10-18, which is protection from demons and witchcraft that want to attack you. Have no unrepented sins in your life. Get rid of the idols in your home, storage room, car, and heart. (Ez. 14:1-11).

Your traumas may surface as you read this book. Claudia Spiro, overwhelmed with the traumas of her Jewish ancestry, was led to let the Lord carry the weight of this persecution. Then peace came. (See Martyr, (and more), Deliverance from Traumas chapter). Do this as you read this book, especially the My Story chapter.

I bind, rebuke, take authority over, and send away, every demon spirit that would use this book to harm or condemn, and not heal and deliver, in the name of Yeshua. Dave Bryan, at Church of Glad Tidings, had an Isaiah 61 Conference in March 2022.[5] He gave 12 aspects of deliverance, the last one being "love." If you don't have love, get it delivered before you try to help someone else.

To cast out the spirits, say, "Go, in the name of Yeshua." Spirits may come out with a manifestation, like a yawn, a cough, or a burp.

If you have never had deliverance, go through Brother Carlos's or Fernando Perez's[6] deliverances several times before tackling these strong principalities and demons over the church and Freemasonry.

Before you begin the deliverance prayers, repent of your sins using the Ten Commandments prayer. (See How I Speak with People Who Need the Savior chapter).

Then pray:

I bring my body, soul, and spirit under the authority of God the Father (Abba Father), God the Son (Yeshua HaMashiach), and God the Holy Spirit (the Ruach HaKodesh). I cover my body, soul, and spirit with the blood of Yeshua (Jesus). Open my understanding, spiritual eyes, and ears to the revelation of the Holy Spirit. Teach me how to use these chapters for my deliverance, that of my family, church, and others. I bind all fears Satan would bring to keep me from receiving deliverance from this book or other sources.

1

The Name of the Savior, Yeshua

Moses said, *"Thou shalt not take the name of the Lord thy God in vain;"* (Ex. 20:7).

When I started witnessing in 1996, I knew the name Yeshua, which is a transliteration of the Hebrew, יֵשׁוּעַ. Though the Savior does answer to other names, it is best to use the name Yeshua and the word for "Savior" in your language. The assurance of eternal life is promised to those who believe in his name.

"That ye may know that ye have eternal life and that ye may believe on the name of the Son of God." (1 John 5:13b).

"Faith in his name" healed the man who was born lame. (Acts 3:16). He was born in Bethlehem, so he must have a Hebrew name. (Micah 5:2 KJV, Mikhah 5:1 CJB; Luke 2:1-7 KJV, CJB).

David H. Stern, in his *Jewish New Testament Commentary*, says the Messiah's name is explained based on what he will do. "He shall save his people from their sins." (Matt. 1:21b KJV). That "in English, saving people from sins" is no more reason for calling someone Jesus than for calling him, Bill or Frank." "Yeshua' is a contraction of the Hebrew name 'Y'hoshua' (English, "Joshua"), which means "YHVH saves." (See References).

Stern says, "Yeshua," no other name, translates as Savior. Other names for the Savior, like Yeshu, originated as an insult and, purposely, a mispronunciation. Some use YahShua or Yahusha for the name of the Savior.

White, the author of *Fossilized Customs, The Pagan Origins of Popular Customs*, says no 'J' existed until the early 1530s in any language. The King James Bible was the first to use the name "Jesus." White says a Greek translation was Iesous. The Society of Jesus, the Jesuits, popularized the use of the name Jesus, closely linked to gods like the Egyptian Isis and the Greek Zeus. "Protestantism picked up this "Jesus" spelling from the Catholic institution, never doubting its origin."[7]

An older man whom I met on the hiking trail was a graduate of a seminary in Denver. He said one of his textbooks verified that the name "Jesus" came from Zeus. I bought him Stern's Jewish New Testament, which gives the name of the Savior as Yeshua. When Yeshua spoke to Apostle Paul, saying, "why are you persecuting me," he spoke Hebrew. So, he must have a Hebrew name. (Acts 26:14-15).

Pastor Eloyse did not use the name Yeshua but knew that Zeus was one name of the Anti-Christ. Robertson indicates that above the altar of Zeus in Pergamos was a hollow bronze bull in which the martyr, Antipas (Rev 2:13), was burned alive. He said the altar was moved to Germany in the 1800s and displayed in Berlin at the Pergamon Museum in 1930. Hitler worshiped Zeus at this altar.[8] [9]

God said his name is *"I Am That I Am."* (Ex. 3:14). Kay, in Nebraska, mailed a page to me saying the *"I Am"* is whatever I need today. Yeshua called his father *"Abba."* (Mark 14:36). Some use *Yahveh* or *Yahweh*. Rabbinic Judaism will not permit speaking the name. They say *"Adonai"* or *"HaShem."* Another name is *Yah*. In that day, we will call upon and exalt his name. (Is. 12:2, 4 NKJV).

"'For Yah, the Lord is my strength and song;'" (Is. 12:2 NKJV).

2

My Story

I read this scripture to my dad on the phone before he died; Instead of shame, I will have a double portion of the land. Everlasting joy shall be mine. (Isaiah 61:7). Johnstone said of Venezuela, "there is a moral breakdown in our society, reflected by many single-parent families. Fatherhood is too often associated with abuse, violence, drunkenness, and irresponsibility. Those who come to Christ often take years to work through the negatives of their past."[10]

I didn't grow up in Venezuela, but it would take me years to work through the negativity of my past. Fathers? What about my mother, uncle, grandpa, and the army men? The Yokefellow church group leader and Dr. M.? This story will unfold as you read further. Since this is my short story, and this book is short, I will explain the bondages and curses I have dealt with and how I have gotten deliverance in my story. I am telling you my story to encourage you and those you minister to. Know that all who desire can receive deliverance.

One woman felt my problems were because I was keeping Jewish traditions. Two women believed it was because I was using the name, Yeshua. Two others believed it was because I was doing spiritual warfare. Two women who hardly knew me commended me for my spiritual warfare. When the prayer

My Story

leader at Beit Tikvah read my life story, she realized my struggle was because I have had so many traumas.

My parent's ancestry was from Germany, the British Isles, and Scandinavia, where Druid witchcraft is practiced, but my families were Lutheran.

My great-great-grandfather and his brothers left Germany one hundred years before Hitler, with a Jewish wife and her family, because of the Catholic and Protestant wars. I learned at a wedding in 2015 that my great-grandmother's name indicated her family are Sephardic Jews.

I was born in the USA. Though the Revolutionary War won our freedom from England, the founders of our country could not free themselves from the Freemasonry of England. Cast out this curse from you and your children if you, and if they were born in any country that has been under England's rule and has freemasonry.

I was born in Nebraska on a witchcraft holiday, December 24th. In 1894, a secret order, Aksarben, Nebraska spelled backward, was formed. Witchcraft spells words backward. A spirit guide and two curses on the firstborn came in at my birth. (See Curses on the Firstborn, Deliverance from Curses chapter).

Anna believed my parents had not reconciled after an argument when I was conceived. Because I became so ill after Christmas 2020 and 2021, Yeshua told me to cast out hatred from my mother and father. I used "The Deliverance List for Familiar Spirits" to eradicate the hatred. (See Appendix G).

I found "The Deliverance List for Familiar Spirits" in 2017. I first used it for deliverance when I was afraid because my older brother had sent me a letter. In other letters, he tried to control me. When I was a child, he and his friend were unkind. At least two times, I came home bleeding.

Being so effective in banishing that fear, I began using this deliverance list for other spiritual bondages. I have used it to free myself from the fear and traumas of 34 persons, some of whom are listed in this story. At times I need to repeat the deliverances. Yeshua has also shown me more deliverances for most of them.

I was baptized as a baby, which brought curses and victimization. Anna delivered these in 1999.

My Mother had learned a strict four-hour feeding schedule for a newborn in nursing school. So, she did not respond to my cries or pick me up until another four hours were up. This was witchcraft. I told her in 1985 that I was having death thoughts, and she admitted she had beaten my older brother and me but none of the younger children. I became ill and almost died, so she prayed for me all night. I had a dream as a child that I was falling but did not hit bottom. I am still delivering myself from those fears when I feel pain or have physical symptoms of illness. (See Childhood Traumas, Deliverance from Traumas chapter). (See the Red Cross, Appendix I). (See Postpartum Depression, Appendix O). (Rejection, See Jonas Clark, References).

Mother was very kind and soft-spoken, although it seems she had Postpartum depression after many pregnancies. I don't remember her beatings, but her prayers after my divorce still benefit me today. After she died in 2002, Yeshua gave me a glimpse of her from the shoulders up. She was young and beautiful, with shoulder-length hair, and she was moving forward.

My father had grown up on a farm. He believed in breaking the spirits of his children, like one breaks a horse, with belt spankings over his knee. Pastor Eloyse said to cast out the death wish under a spirit called Oblivio that attacks the brain.

I also experienced abandonment by my father, though he was home every night, unless he was at a Bible camp or a church convention. This emotional rejection caused me to be vulnerable to "False Fathers" as a child and throughout my young adult years. (See Beelzebub, 80-list, Appendix E).

There was victimization by men of the army who stayed at our country parsonage to open the roads after a snowstorm and by men remodeling the church who were also there. I was also traumatized at Bible camps, and by others I already mentioned.

My cousin and I spoke on the phone in 1991. From what she said her father had confessed, our ancestors had wanted children to sleep together. My father disapproved of this incest; he caught us children playing doctor and spanked us. My cousin believes her father got to my mother. He had to work in South America because of his behavior towards women. I think he perpetrated on three generations in our family. But my sister had an Assembly of God pastor pray with him before he died. He is in heaven. (See Luther, Anti-Semitism, Deliverance from Curses chapter).

However, on December 18th, 2018, a woman I met at a Friday evening home worship prayed for me. She said Jesus showed her a farm and rolling hills. She also told me that she saw Jesus holding me like his little lamb. I told her that was where I lived the first eight years of my life. Because Yeshua was there to hold me, I am alive today. She also counseled me as we edited My Story chapter. My first memories are of the Sunday school teacher writing on the blackboard what Yeshua said.

"I am the door. I am the good shepherd."

(John 10:9a, 11a).

Every summer, we went to a family Bible camp that I loved. There were morning classes, afternoon teaching in the chapel, swimming, and evening services in the huge tabernacle.

My mom and dad got the Holy Spirit in 1962. This changed the family, but I was away at high school.

My Father's Induction into the Boy Scout Order of the Arrow

In 1959, my father was inducted into the Boy Scout Order of the Arrow (OA). My mother, six siblings, and I attended this campfire ceremony, but I am the only one who remembers it. There was drumming, nearly naked scoutmasters wearing only huge eagle feather headdresses and loincloths, dancing around the campfire, chanting, "wow, wow, and wow." The drums and this chant are both Native American and African. I hear them in churches, and I don't like them. I still deliver these spirits out of me and proxy them in prayer out of my family because my present husband was also inducted into this order. I then found myself bonding with persons with strong scouting and freemason bondages, later learning that scouting is freemason in origin. (See Worship of the Gods of Indigenous Peoples, Have No Other Gods chapter).

My Father did not believe in dancing, drinking alcohol, playing cards, using illegal drugs, smoking, or watching terrible TV programs. He only had one girlfriend all his life, my mother. In 2005, the summer before he died, he said he wished he had never been in that order.

This pagan Boy Scout ceremony, as well as the curses from infant baptism, and childhood molestations, brought trouble in our teen and adult years. Mistreatment of children breaks God's heart.

After my father's initiation into this witchcraft Scouting order, three predators in one town victimized my family. I tried to tell my mother about the policeman's son who entered our basement. She said he was my brother's friend and discounted my concern. The only one, my parents, became aware of got 15 years behind bars. Then my father asked to be moved to a different parish, but we were still not safe. A man asked my father if a brother could come and work for him. My brother withstood him when he tried to molest him.

In keeping with the freemason Egyptian goddess, Isis, my sisters kept these secrets; they could not recognize the evil or speak up and defend themselves. I could not get over these attacks on my sisters. I thought about it every day. I recently was triggered on a witches' sabbath, fearing that this man, though he is deceased, would come and rape my sisters. (See Appendix A).

Failure, Sorrow, and Salvation

I went to Lutheran High Schools in two different cities and graduated as a salutatorian. I failed at my first attempt to be a nurse. Then again, when my first child was a baby, I withdrew from nurses' training when we eventually moved.

A Ouija board told me the name of my first husband. Severe deprivations and perversions in this marriage set me up for the Yokefellow church group leader. A diabolical alliance between my husband and the group leader nearly destroyed me. My husband's boss had him join the Jaycees; a "Brotherhood" connected to the freemasons. Later, this group leader became a Shriner in Freemasonry.

My relationship with the Yokefellow church group leader caused me to withdraw from 3 women's organizations where I held offices. He gave me a book to read, written by a prostitute. He did not need to because Krodeus' spirits and sexual addiction can come with these sexual betrayals. (See The Deliverance List for Familiar Spirits, Appendix G).

He blackmailed me with the threat of losing my children if I didn't agree to mate-swapping. I blocked the blackmail out until 1990.

I dropped out after the third year in my third attempt to be a nurse, but I still dream of reentering nursing school. The good that came from this is my children, and I started going to the Assembly of God church. I created a sign and put it on our refrigerator.

"Christ in (Me), the Hope of Glory." (Col. 1:27b)

I learned ten years later that I had been raped under hypnosis during 14 sessions with a psychologist, Dr. M., my Abnormal Psychology instructor. He threatened to kill my children and me if I told a soul. When I called the Nebraska Psychological Association, he had just lost his license. (See and cast out Beelzebub, false father, 80-list, Appendix E).

I went forward to be 'saved' four times from 1961 to 1996 and received immersion baptisms in 1983 and 1984.

Beginning of Deliverance, Disability, and Remarriage

I discovered that many people who have been abused as a child were then victimized in marriages and other relationships. Herman verified this, saying they may also harm themself. Men that were abused as children are more apt to abuse others.[11]

I could not protect myself. Due to continued revictimization in Nebraska, my brother helped me move to Colorado for deliverance in 1983. I cleaned houses, lived, and worked in Pastor Eloyse's home, and had one other part-time job.

Pastor Eloyse invited Pastor Tom Fritch to speak on witnessing at a summer camp. He said he always complimented the person he was witnessing to.[12] I would pattern my witnessing after him. I had three-year workplace exposure to an organic solvent. I received disability in 1990 and moved away from CLF.

Pastor Fritch officiated at the wedding of my second husband and me in 1991.

To ignore many warnings is typical of abused persons. (1 Cor. 10:13). Every time I ignored a warning, it brought another trauma. I joined two other women traumatized by psychiatric professionals and formed a support group in an Arvada church for deliverance and healing. The pastor visited our group a few times and taught us. In August 1996, Bill Fay taught on witnessing at the same Arvada church.[13] I was thrilled by the verse he used. For seven years, I used Fay's method of witnessing, much on the city bus.

> "These things have I written unto you that believe on the name of the Son of God; that ye may know that ye have eternal life."
>
> (1 John 5:13a).

My Deliverance from Confirmation, Infant Baptism, and Freemason Bondages

One Sabbath in 1998, I felt that I should return to CLF. In 1999, Anna, my deliverance counselor, was home ill when I came for counseling. She instructed me, over the phone, to pray in tongues for five minutes and then call her several times in a row. When I did this, I learned that a spirit of perfection had come in when I was confirmed. Then, in many weekly sessions, Anna ministered deliverance to me from confirmation, infant baptism, freemason bondages, and a demonic trinity over my family. (See Luther, Antisemitism, Deliverance from Curses chapter).

After getting these deliverances from curses and secret orders, I got a new heart and a new spirit. (Ezek. 36:26-27a. NKJV; Rom. 11:15). I knew my name was written in heaven. I didn't need to respond to "altar calls" any longer.

> "Behold, I give unto you power to tread on serpents and scorpions, and over all the power of the enemy: and nothing shall by any means hurt you. Notwithstanding in this rejoice not, that the spirits are subject unto you; but rather rejoice, because your names are written in heaven."
>
> (Luke 10:19-20).

Many Receive the Savior

In 2003, Yeshua taught me different questions to ask as I witnessed, but I retained two of Fay's questions. "Do you believe there is a heaven and a hell? And, where will you go when you die?" Many more people began to say "yes," to the Savior. Hispanic persons and the homeless were more apt to say, "yes." I stopped counting in April 2010, at over 1,500. Many had also renounced their infant baptism. I became so busy witnessing that I gave up work in Right to Life and my watercolor class.

Learning a Curse Comes in With Infant Baptism

In 2008, I was waiting for the city bus to go home but decided to return to the CLF office. Anna was cleaning out her desk, which revealed a deliverance pattern I had never seen. I was shocked to see that a curse had come into me from infant baptism, which I passed to my children. (See Infant Baptism, Have no other God's chapter).

Opposition to the Gospel

There is a war against the gospel. (Matthew 24:9-14). Yeshua warned us that we would suffer if we did what he told us to do. But we should not be offended. (Mark 10:29-30; John 16:1-3; 2 Tim. 3:12). People hate God but can't kill him, so they attack Jewish people and believers, especially those that bring the good news. (Ex. 20:5; John 15:20).

Pray for angels to help and protect you as you witness.

"Are they not all ministering spirits, sent forth to minister for them who shall be heirs of salvation?" (Heb. 1:14).

A Missionary family was going to a predominantly Catholic country. I tried to tell the wife that the people needed deliverance from infant baptism bondages, but the pastor interrupted me and said I could not speak to her. I later learned that the Catholic church secretly founded this church, but I doubt the pastor was aware of this. Typhon opposes the deliverance minister. (See Deliverance from Curses chapter).

I got permission from the pastor in a church in Mexico to witness after the service, but a man with a religious spirit stopped me. The same occurred at a December party in a park for poor people who live on the hill.

"*And a man's foes shall be they of his own household.*" (Matt. 10:36).

Some of my family members don't want me to evangelize in their neighborhoods. Several others will not allow me to speak to them or read the Bible to my grandson.

In Mexico, my father-in-law and his neighbor opposed my witnessing to the maids and gardeners as they came to work. Ten years later, my mother-in-law and the neighbor's wife died from cancer. The doctor said my mother-in-law had cancer for ten years. (Deut. 7:15). Now, I immediately remit the sins of these persons who oppose my witness because I don't want them to get cancer. (See Remitting Sins chapter).

In December 2012, I called my mother-in-law and said that Yeshua could heal her of insomnia. She had not learned she had cancer. She said "yes" to the Savior and died in May. A song came to me, "Rise, Shine, Give God Glory," when I asked Yeshua if she was in heaven. I knew she was. My Father-in-law's nurse and caregiver took him to church. I believe he accepted the Savior.

Dr. Rebecca Brown, author of *He Came to Set the Captives Free*, said the witches were trying to kill her in the hospital where she did her internship. Witnessing was prohibited. The Gideon Bibles were removed, and there was no chaplain. Ministers were "forbidden to visit with anyone except their parishioners."[14] After graduation, she returned to the hospital to deliver Elaine, the head witch, who became her patient.[15]

I have found these same restrictions in some medical facilities, especially assisted living, nursing homes, and other facilities for the mentally ill. But many medical personnel will receive my literature. Except in Hindu, communist, or Islamic countries, one should be able to witness freely on public sidewalks and in public parks. Christian legal groups may defend you if you are arrested for witnessing in these places.

3

The Spanish Inquisition
and It's Effect Today

We have been immersed in worldly culture, even in our place of worship, and forced to worship other gods. David said there was a curse on the children of men, who drove him from his land and forced him to worship other gods as he hid from King Saul. (1 Sam. 26:19).

Not long after Yeshua returned to heaven, all believers were forbidden from keeping the biblical feasts and sabbaths. Sanchez documents that for thousands of years, lies have propagated hatred of the Jewish people, especially through the false doctrines of Replacement Theology and Kingdom Now.[16]

The Sephardic Jewish people

Dell Sanchez came to Denver several times and was on Sid Roth's Television program.[17] I learned that the Sephardic Jewish people are from the southern kingdom, the tribes of Judah and Benjamin, that were taken captive to Babylon.[18] Solomon's sin caused a separation of the 12 tribes of Jacob. The ten northern tribes of Israel worshipped false gods and were scattered into Assyria. (1 Kings 11:1-13;2 Kings 17:6).

In addition to the Sephardic Jewish people, there are also Ashkennazi and Ethiopian Jewish people. The Lord said, *"so shall your seed and our name remain."* (Is. 66:22).

Sanchez brought our attention to the yet unfulfilled prophecy of Obadiah 20.

> "The exiles from Yerushalayim in S'farad (Spain) will repossess the cities in the Negev." (Southern Israel). (Obadiah 20, CJB).

Biblical references to Spain, Tharshish, or Tarshish are 1 Kings 10:22, Jonah 1:3, and Romans 15:24.

In 1492, Jewish people in Spain had to convert to Catholicism or leave Spain. To escape this Spanish Inquisition, Sanchez said some went to Northern Africa, Europe, Turkey, and Israel. Some came to the New World with Christopher Columbus, Cortez, and Carvajal. They went to the Caribbean islands, the northern coast of South America, and the east coast of Central America.[19]

Sanchez said those who escaped the Spanish Inquisition were safe in the New World for less than thirty years. When the Inquisition arrived, they were again forced to baptize their babies, pray to Mary, and eat pork.[20] Communities were separated, and families were forced to intermarry with the indigenous peoples. Many Hispanic people I speak with in Colorado say they are half American Indian. (See Worship of the Gods of Indigenous Peoples, Have No Other Gods chapter).

Johnson says 341,000 were killed in the Spanish Inquisition. Among the tortures, about ten percent were burned alive. Especially targeted were those who were practicing a Jewish lifestyle in secret.[21]

A homeless veteran of the Iraq and Afghanistan war said his family came with Cortez in 1550. He knew about torture on the rack and that some had a secret room to worship in.

All Jewish people, not just the Sephardic Jews, have suffered. Two Hispanics told me last week how they are hated and mistreated. Some accepted sprinkling baptism, hoping to halt the persecution against them.

Sanchez believes one-fifth of the Hispanics in the Western Hemisphere are descendants of Sephardic Anusim Jews.[22] Anusim means being forced (to be Catholic). Mandryk said that many Hispanic Catholics in the USA today are evangelicals, and nearly fifty percent are Charismatic.[23]

I found a four-hour Sunday afternoon service at a Hispanic church while visiting my parents. The pastor came to visit my father and then spoke at my father's funeral. Looking for a church like this, I have attended various Hispanic churches here and in Mexico.

We are to go to the Jewish people first. (Rom. 1:16). A rider on the Denver city bus asked me why I was only speaking with the Hispanics.

Most Spanish Jewish people are still ignorant of or hiding the secret of their Jewish identity. A young woman said that her mother grabbed the Spanish Jew literature I gave her, terrified that her family would learn that they were Jewish.

Why the terror? Because Nury Rivera, the widow of Alberto Rivera, a former Jesuit priest, said the Inquisitions have never ended.[24]

I told a young Hispanic mother about Christian Spanish television programs. She was so grateful that she gave me the doll she had received when her baby was baptized!

Another Hispanic neighbor knew she was Jewish but wouldn't give up her belief in saints, infant baptism, or catechism. She wanted to know about curses and needed deliverance from traumas. She repented of her sins, using the Ten Commandments, accepted Yeshua's blood to wash them, and is now in heaven. We read verses on the biblical feasts, in addition to 1 Peter 1:18-19 and John 3:1-17.

A man in a clinic waiting room said that he cried out to God, and his life was spared, though he lost part of a leg in Vietnam. While we waited to see the doctors, I let him read Sanchez's book, *The Last Exodus*. Having found the identity of his people, The Spanish Jews, he accepted the Savior and asked for prayer for his girlfriend and her daughter.

My in-laws bought a home in Mexico in 1999. I walked around a bar, doing spiritual warfare. The following year, the manager wanted literature for each of his employees!

At my visit in 2006, eleven persons in Mexico repented of their sins, and two renounced their Catholic bondages. I gave Bibles to three of them.

On a Mission trip to Mexico in 2017, with a pastor and three other persons, I ministered deliverance to a woman at a mental hospital.[25] I had a bilingual Bible, which helped me communicate with her, and I gave her a Bible and wrote down verses for her to read after I left.

The descendants of these people need deliverance that I received in 1999 from infant baptism, catechism, and freemasonry, and they need deliverance from many traumatic experiences.

Dr. Sanchez said a curse had come on the Sephardic Jews from the Inquisition.[26]

I left one Hispanic church because the pastor did not believe that his people could have curses that would prevent them from knowing they had eternal life.

4

Remitting Sins

Yeshua has the power to forgive sins and said we would do greater works than he did. (Matt. 9:6; John 14:12). Rexa Daniels, the assistant pastor at CLF, taught about "remitting sins" on October 21, 1987.

Yeshua said, *"Whosoever sins ye remit, (forgive) they are remitted unto them."* (John 20:23a).

In 1987, I began remitting the sins of my family in prayer. These prayers would be crucial for my Father's and my granddaughter's entrance into heaven. I used the Ten Commandments, Daniel chapter 9, and other scriptures to remit sins.

After my mother died in 2002, I continued to visit Dad for three weeks at a time. Yeshua would show me the spiritual warfare needed in the house and the yard, and I would also call Anna for advice. My Father and I would pray and sing, even over the phone, when I was in Denver. And we would study the Bible together. We even rode with a friend to a Messianic congregation. I feel I bonded with him, spiritually, more than anyone in my lifetime. Though my parents were saved at a youth Bible camp, I was concerned about my father's salvation because he had baptized babies in the Lutheran church. (See Infant Baptism, Have No Other Gods chapter).

I received deliverance from infant baptism in 1999. At the end of his life, Dad knew infant baptism and Confirmation were not the way to heaven, but, having dementia, he could not repent for having baptized babies. In January 2006, I read to him from Isaiah 61:1-3 & v.7 over the phone.

> *"The Spirit of the Lord God is upon Me Because the Lord has anointed Me To preach good tidings to the poor; He has sent Me to heal the brokenhearted, ... Instead of your shame you shall have double honor, ... Everlasting joy shall be theirs."* (Isaiah 61:1a, 7a, c. NKJV).

I also read him the best verse I could find about the blood of the Messiah.

> *"You should be aware that the ransom paid to free you from the worthless way of life which your fathers passed on to you did not consist of anything perishable like silver or gold; on the contrary, it was the costly bloody sacrificial death of the Messiah, as of a lamb without defect or spot."* (1 Peter 1:18-19 CJB).

Dad knew about the blood of Jesus to wash his sins away. He responded with a chorus. "What can wash away my sin? Nothing but the blood of Jesus."[27]

Anna and I met the next three Tuesdays to pray for him. During the first week, we spent several hours asking Jesus to forgive him for all his sins, including baptizing babies. Then a brother caring for him said he had a dream. Jesus came to him and told him that his sins had been forgiven. It had something to do with his daughter, Ruth. Thank you, Yeshua.

My granddaughter is also in heaven because I remitted her sins as I was remitting the sins of the whole family.

Don't Remit a "Sin unto Death"

> *"If anyone sees his brother committing a sin that does not lead to death, he will ask, and God will give him life for those whose sinning does not lead to death. There is sin that does*

lead to death; I am not saying he should pray about that." (1 John 5:16 CJB)

What is a sin unto death? 1 Corinthians 6:9-11 and Revelations 21:8 list sins, some of them in the Ten Commandments, adding sorcery, fornication, drunkenness, and being effeminate or fearful. The only unforgivable sin is blasphemy against the Holy Spirit. (Mark 3:28-29). All other sins can be forgiven, but from a sin that leads to death, I believe the person needs to repent and stop the sin themself.

Do Christians Need to Repent?

Both John the Baptist and Yeshua came, preaching;

"Repent, for the kingdom of heaven is at hand." (Matt. 3:2; 4:17 NKJV)

In 1985, my father sent me a letter saying, "God is calling us to repent because he loves us." If one does not repent before taking communion, one could become weak, sick, and die. (1 Cor. 11:30).

If you have a conscience and read the Bible, the Holy Spirit will show you what sins you must repent.

Unrepented sin is serious. For two weeks, the children in Baker's orphanage in China got trips to heaven without dying and saw visions of demons and hell. They saw the death of a professing Christian who had not truly repented. The demons bound him before he was entirely out of his body, and "in terror, he was dragged and pushed into hell." [28] But there is a demonic blockage to repentance.

In the 6 *Big Big Big Angels* book, a boy was repenting for fighting with another boy when he died in a car accident and went to heaven. (See References).

5

Know You Have Eternal Life
and Questionnaire

I want people to be sure of going to heaven when they die. Apostle John speaks of this as "eternal life." Knowing one has eternal life and knowing the name of the Savior are both important.

> "These things have I written unto you that believe on the name of the Son of God; that ye may know that ye have eternal life." (1 John 5:13a).

In *They Thought for Themselves*, Sharon Allen is a Jewish person who came to believe in the Savior. Commenting on Allen's story, Sid Roth says that if one is not sure of going to heaven before they die, their fate is everlasting abhorrence![29]

The Promise of a Savior

Lucifer was expelled from heaven because of his rebellion against God. (Is. 14:12-23 KJV, or NKJV).

> "Woe to the inhabiters of the earth and the sea! For the devil is come down unto you, having great wrath, because he knoweth that he hath but a short time." (Rev. 12:12b)

Lucifer keeps people in prison. (Is.14:17). Yeshua sets us free. (Is. 61:1, Luke 4:18)

His name was changed to Satan. (Luke 10:18).

> "The thief (Satan) cometh not, but for to steal, and to kill, and to destroy: I am come that they might have

life and that they might have it more abundantly."
(John 10:10). (Also see Isaiah 14:12-21).

In Genesis 3:15, God promised that he would send the Savior who would bruise the head of the serpent, Satan.

"But when the fulness of the time was come, God sent forth his Son, made of a woman, made under the law, To redeem them that were under the law, that we might receive the adoption of sons." (Gal. 4:4-5).

"For God so loved the world, that he gave his only begotten Son, that whosoever believeth in him should not perish, but have everlasting life. For God sent not his Son into the world to condemn the world; but that the world through him might be saved." (John 3:16-17). (Also, see Rom. 10:9).

The religious leaders influenced many against Yeshua. (Mark 3:1-6; John 11:45-53).

He came to his own, and his own received him not. (John 1:11)

The multitude took a curse on themselves, calling for Yeshua's crucifixion.

All the people ... said, "his blood be on us, and on our children." (Matt. 27:25).

Peter, calling for their repentance, said, "the promise is unto you and to your children." (Acts 2:38-39; Isaiah 54:13).

"(Yeshua) will have all men to be saved, and to come unto the knowledge of the truth." (1 Tim. 2:3b,4).

What Yeshua Commanded Us to Do

"And this gospel of the kingdom shall be preached in all the world for a witness unto all nations; and then shall the end come." (Matt. 24:14)

Yeshua said, "occupy till I come." (Luke 19:13b). To me, occupy means preaching the gospel. (Mark 16:15-18, John 20:21).

> "To wit, that God was in Christ, reconciling the world unto himself, not imputing their trespasses unto them; and hath committed unto us the word of reconciliation." (2 Cor 5:19).

Yeshua commands us to go with the gospel and cast out demons. Because believers, for generations, have not obeyed, families, churches, cities, states, and our countries are not healthy. Many are even atheists or worship Satan.

Concern about Curses

In 1987, I began remitting the sins of my family. Still, more recently, I have become concerned about exposing and delivering curses, which bring destruction and illness that severely affect even believers. I was impressed to stand against curses over close family members after going to bed one Sunday night. The following morning my son called, saying my grandson had no injuries, though his car was totaled after sliding off the interstate and hitting a tree. Thank you, Yeshua.

Tom Horn documents that the sacraments of the church are sorcery. (Rev. 18:23). (See Infant Baptism, Have No Other Gods chapter).

Park said sorcery from puppetry, rock music, magic, and other devices of Satan, blinds the eyes, dulls the ears, and sears the conscience so that people will defend these lies. She said the Holy Spirit opens their understanding to the destructive forces in these works. (Heb. 5:11; 1 Tim 4:2).[30]

This sorcery brings curses that keep people in the church from being assured of going to heaven, though they know that Yeshua died for their sins.

I was ushered out of a large sabbath ministry after offering literature to a woman in the restroom. The security guard said, of being sure of going to heaven when one dies, "that is a private matter."

I accessed four churches and found at best, only half were sure of going to heaven. (See Addendum II, The Answer to my Four Questions in Four Hispanic Churches and One Other Church). (See Spiritual Death, Have No Other Gods chapter).

Difficulty Communicating My Concerns

It has been difficult for me to relay these insights. I called a deliverance minister in 2013, asking if his deliverance conference would be online. I also told him that some persons in the church are not sure about going to heaven. He blamed me! I was shocked!

A deliverance leader in 2013 agreed that infant baptism needed to be delivered but did not implement it. Two deliverance ministers and two Messianic leaders rejected the need for deliverance from infant baptism. But one of them raised a man from the dead, and another delivered a witch from Canada who came to Denver.

> *"Then said Jesus, Father, forgive them; for they know not what they do."* (Luke 23:34a)

Know You Have Eternal Life. Questionnaire

You may print this out for your church or group to answer. It is better to question orally and individually.

Your name. _____

Telephone. _____

Address. _____
_____

The date. _____/_____/_____

I want you to be sure you will go to heaven when you die.

What did the Savior do 2000 years ago so that you can go to heaven?

_____
_____
_____

Do you believe that there is a heaven and a hell? Yes, or No.

Where do you believe your soul and spirit will go when you die?

_____

If you say 'to heaven,' why will you go to heaven?

_____
_____

(I don't ask the questions below as I witness, but it may be appropriate for a church or study group.)

Do you read your Bible? Yes, or no?

When? _____
_____

Did you receive the Holy Spirit and speak with other tongues? (Acts 2:4; 19:6). Yes, or no?

Do you often pray or sing in tongues? Yes, or no? (1 Cor. 14:15).

Do you witness about the Savior? Yes, or no?

When? _____

I want you to have the right answer for going to heaven when you die and to know you have eternal life.

If you are unsure about going to heaven, repent of your sins and say "yes" to the Savior and his blood to wash your sins, and then look for someone to help you with deliverances.

There may be some sins that are difficult to stop. You may need deliverance from curses like infant baptism, Cub, Boy or Girl Scouts, or Freemasonry. You may have traumas or bondages from your own sins, your own family, or your spouse's family. Many people go to good churches but are unsure about going to heaven when they die. (Mark 16:15-20, 1 John 5:13).

Pastor or Leader: It is best to ask these questions personally and minister immediately to the person with the wrong reason for going to heaven. You may not reencounter these same persons. However, this person likely needs much counsel and deliverance.

6

The Biblical Feasts and Sabbaths are for Today

Why are these feasts in a book about salvation? I need to show you the biblical feast days before I show you that, shockingly, the holidays the church observes are rooted in witchcraft.

Yeshua came to fulfill the law, not to abolish it. (Matt. 5:17). He fulfilled all the feasts except the Feast of Trumpets.

The Sabbath Leviticus 23:1-3

"Then God blessed the seventh day and sanctified it because in it He rested from all His work which God had created and made." (Gen. 2:1-3 NKJV; Ex. 20:8-11)

"Six days shall work be done: but the seventh day is the sabbath of rest, a holy convocation; ye shall do no work therein: it is the sabbath of the Lord in all your dwellings." (Lev. 23:3, See also Is. 66:23)

The biblical feasts have seven additional sabbaths. (Ex. 20:8; Lev. 23; John 14:15).

Many believe that Yeshua rose from the tomb on Easter Sunday, beginning Sunday worship. However, Bacchiocchi said, "the church of Rome has been primarily responsible for the institution of Sunday observance."[31]

Apostle Paul preached on the Sabbath. (Acts 13:14, 42, 44, 17:2, 18:4). He and Silas went to a women's Sabbath prayer meeting. (Acts 16:13-15)

Preparation Days for a Sabbath

In the lifestyle of a family who keeps the Sabbath, preparation days before the sabbath are used to prepare food, so no cooking is done on the Sabbath. Cleaning and Laundry have also been done before the Sabbath. (Luke 23:54; John 19:14).

Closing of the Sabbath Meetings

Yeshua opposed the severe laws of the religious leaders. He did heal some persons on the Sabbath. But usually, most were brought for deliverance and healing at the close of the Sabbath. (Matt. 8:16-17; Mark 1:32-34).

The story in Acts 20:7-12 has been used to validate Sunday worship wrongly. It was not Sunday morning; it was the evening of the first day of the week at the closing of the Sabbath when the disciples gathered to break bread, and many lamps had been lit. Eutychus fell asleep and fell from the third-story window. Paul restored him to life, then preached until morning and departed.

Some Jewish people have parties at the close of the Sabbath, called Havurahs, Le Havdil, or Havdalah's.

> "So let no one judge you in food or drink, or regarding a festival or a new moon or sabbaths, which are a shadow of things to come, but the substance is of Christ." (Col. 2:16-17 NKJV)

The Spring Feasts

On the first Passover in Egypt, the blood of the Passover lamb on the doorpost caused the angel of death to pass over the homes of the Jewish people, so their firstborns were not killed.

The Lord told Moses that Passover would fall in the first month of the year, not January or the Feast of Trumpets in the fall, as Rabbinic Judaism declares.

The Feast of Unleavened Bread coincides with Passover. (Lev. 23:4-8; Ex. 12:17, 39). Leaven speaks of sin. (1 Cor. 5:7-8). Yeshua became the sinless sacrifice for sin, the Passover lamb. (Ex. 12:13, 23, 29; Is.53:7; 1 Peter 1:16-19).

At this feast, sing Messianic songs or "When I See the Blood, I will Pass Over You."

Yeshua rose from the tomb on the Feast of First Fruits. (1 Cor. 15:20). The Feast of First Fruits is the only feast with no holy convocations or gathering to worship (Lev. 23:9-14), but the church observes Easter Sunday.

Yeshua had to be in the tomb for three days and nights. He could not have been crucified on Good Friday and raised on Easter Sunday.

> *"For as Jonas was three days and three nights in the whale's belly; so shall the Son of man be three days and three nights in the heart of the earth."* (Matt. 12:40)

He was put in the tomb on the 14th day of Nissan, the first month of the Hebrew calendar. Nissan 15 is the first of the two extra sabbath days during Passover. (Lev. 23:5). He was crucified on a Wednesday and rose just as the seventh day Sabbath ended. In the Bible and the Hebrew calendar, days begin and end at sunset. (Gen. 1:5).

Apostle John validates this. After his resurrection, it was dark, just after sunset, at the close of the Sabbath, on the first day of the week, when Yeshua appeared to Mary (Miryam) and then the disciples. So, Mary did not recognize him. (John 20:1, 19)

Hansen cites Holmgren[32] claiming a difference between the beginning of a day for the Jewish people as compared to the Greeks led to a mistranslation of Matthew 28:1 and Mark 16:2 in the KJV. Hansen believes that "Yeshua was resurrected just as the (seventh day) Sabbath ended and the Festival of First Fruits began." He said the Messiah's death, burial, and resurrection on the 3rd day are part of the gospel that saves us. (1 Cor. 15:1-4).[33] (Matt. 12:40).

Blood On the Mercy Seat

On the Fall feast of the Day of Atonement, Yom Kippur, the High Priest, entered the Holy of Holies with the blood of a bullock and then blood of a goat, which he sprinkled on the Ark of the Covenant. (Lev. 16:2-34; Heb 9:7). Yeshua became our high priest and offered his body and blood for our sin. (Heb. 10:10. See also vs. 1 - 22). The sins of the people were also placed on the head of a scapegoat and it was sent into the wilderness. (Lev. 16:10). Our sins were placed on Yeshua. Is. 53:3-12).

Ron Wyatt, an anesthesiologist, and archeologist found the original Ark of the Covenant in a cave below mount calvary, where Jeremiah had hidden it before the temple's destruction 600 years earlier. 2 Maccabees 2:4-8 refers to Jeremiah hiding the ark but gives the wrong location. Wyatt said the earthquake of Matthew 27:50-52 opened a crevice under the cross that allowed Yeshua's blood, from his pierced side (John 19:34), to descend 20 feet onto the Ark of the Covenant. The angels guarding the ark told Wyatt to have the blood analyzed in a lab. The lab technicians said his blood is alive.[34] It can still wash away our sins. (1 Peter 1:18-19).

I believe the ark in Ethiopia is a duplicate ark Solomon made for the Queen of Sheba.

The Feast of Weeks, Pentecost Leviticus 23:15-22

Seven weeks plus one day leads to Shavuot, Pentecost.

Yeshua went up to heaven 40 days after he rose from the dead. (Acts 1:3). His followers waited in the upper room until God the Father sent down the Holy Spirit ten days later. (Luke 24:49; Acts 1:4 - 15, Acts 2). The gospel went out to the world after the Holy Spirit came down, prophesized in Joel 2:28-32. (Yo'el 3:1-5 CJB).

Apostle Paul celebrated the feasts of unleavened bread and Pentecost. (Acts 20:6, 16; 1 Cor. 16:8).

The Fall Feasts

The Feast of Trumpets Leviticus 23:23-25,1 Thessalonians 4:16-17

I believe the souls and spirits of repentant believers at death go to heaven, but their bones will be raised when they hear Yeshua's voice and the trumpet blows. This will likely be at the Feast of Trumpets before the great tribulation begins. Therefore, cremation is wrong. (2 Cor. 5:8; John 5:28-29; 1 Thess. 4:16-19). Some wrongly believe their soul sleeps, waiting for Judgement. For this feast sing, "When the Roll is called up Yonder, I'll be there."

The Day of Atonement Leviticus 23:26-32

(See Wyatt, above).

The Feast of Tabernacles, Sukkoth Leviticus 23:33-43

Many prophecies about the end times are only partially or not yet fulfilled. Messianic congregations celebrate Yeshua's first coming at the Feast of Tabernacles. His second coming will be fulfilled at the Feast of Tabernacles when he comes to tabernacle among us. (John 1:14; Rev. 21:3). Then, he will set up his government in Yerushalayim. (Obadiah 15; Rev. 19:11 - 20:6 KJV, CJB).

Those nations who do not come to Jerusalem to celebrate the Feast of Tabernacles when Yeshua is reigning in the

Millenium will get no rain. (Zech, 14:16-19). (Also, see John 7:2, 37 – 39)

Purim is celebrated just before Passover. Queen Esther declared a fast so she could ask the king to save her people. Then the Jewish people were allowed to gather and fight against those who wanted to destroy them. (Esther 4:15-16, 8:11). The nation of Israel is forced to physically fight against her enemies. But some believers like myself are engaged in spiritually waring against Satan and his host.

This is a guide for spiritual warfare. We are to fight spiritually because Satan wants to destroy us and take us to hell. Deborah was a judge and a warrior. The angel of the Lord pronounced a curse on Meroz, who did not join Deborah in the battle. (Judges 5:23). However, we are not to curse anyone today.

Concerns about Messianic Judaism borrowing from Rabbinic Judaism

I am concerned about mixtures in both the Sunday and the Sabbath meetings. I am not advocating that one convert to Rabbinic Judaism or display or wear a six-pointed star. (See the six-pointed star, Symbols and Emblems that bring curses chapter). Some other concerns I have with Messianic worship are:

Prayers to the "King of the Universe." The word, Universe, is not in the Bible.

The church calls Shavuot, Pentecost. When some congregations celebrate Shavuot, they ignore that the Holy Spirit came on Shavuot and only continue to celebrate the Ten Commandments and other laws. (Exodus 19, 20, and more).

Some congregations use the long Al Chet prayer from Rabbinic Judaism to confess sins at Yom Kippur. I believe they should use the Ten Commandments and verses out of the New Testament. One couple left Messianic Judaism because of a false doctrine at a Yom Kippur service.

In one Messianic congregation Sabbath class, we studied the Kabbalah. Park, Stevens, and Kitchen identify that Kabbalah, Jewish Mysticism, is also used in Freemasonry. Some congregations borrow from Rabbinic Judaism, "Kabbalat Shabbat," receiving the Sabbath.

Ideally, a messianic congregation would follow Yeshua and not use the six-pointed star, the Kabbalah, and unbiblical Rabbinic laws. I love Hebrew songs and Israeli dance. Victoria, from the 6 Big Big Big Angels book, said she learned the same Hebrew songs sung at messianic congregations when she was in heaven. (See References).

The Mikvah

The Jewish people observed biblical health laws, taking an immersion bath before entering the temple, to not die or defile the tabernacle. (Lev. 15:31). The Torah instructs a man and woman to bathe after intimacy and be unclean until evening. (Lev. 15:18). However, it has become a custom for a Jewish woman to take a ritual bath, a Mikvah, seven days after her menstruation ceases. (Lev. 15:19).

Laws for Foods

Kosher laws based on Exodus 23:19 are so strict that some Jewish people have become vegetarians. The Bible tells us not to eat unclean food like pork and shellfish. (Lev. 11, see also Is. 66:17).). We are not to eat meat with fat and blood in it. My husband learned to broil thin strips of beef or ground beef and turkey patties until they were well done. He does not turn the meat over—the fat and blood drip into the broiler pan. (Lev. 7:23, 25-27; Acts 15:20). The Passover lamb was roasted. (Ex.12:8-9). A Messianic woman from Norway taught me to soak a whole chicken in salt water a day before roasting it.

7

Have No Other Gods

To discern whether I should go for deliverance in a church with Sunday and Sabbath services, I walked around the building seven times doing spiritual warfare. Then, Yeshua revealed to me that the Sunday church is a secret order.

All the secrets will be made known. (Luke 8:17). We are to expose the "unfruitful works of darkness." (Eph. 5:11b).

We have worshiped in ignorance. The priests, the congregation, and rulers offered sacrifices for sins they had committed in ignorance. (Lev. 4; Heb. 9:7).

> "Return unto me, and I will return unto you, saith the Lord of hosts." (Mal. 3:7b).

Use the text in this chapter as a guide for delivering yourself or others. At CLF I learned to underline and check off my deliverances.

What is a Secret Order?

Park said, "people learned in secret signs and passwords, hand grips, vows, and rituals, are under the bondage of Lucifer." "The devil knows that by getting you to vow to secrecy to the works of darkness, he has you under his dominion."[35]

Lucifer has secret signs. God's signs are not secret. His Words. (Deut. 6:4-8). The Sabbath. (Ezek. 20:12, 20).

Deliverance, speaking in tongues, protection, and healing are signs of a believer. (Mark 16:17-20, Acts 2:22).

I grew up in a secret order, the Lutheran church. We had vows (catechism and marriage), and rituals (liturgy and sacraments), and we shook hands with the pastor as we exited the church. We also had unbiblical doctrines, symbols, and holidays. We didn't know about the seventh day Sabbath.

Anna delivered me in 1999, but these deliverances were not retained in the CLF files. In this chapter and this book, I have brought together information from several sources that may assist you, as you find that you or other persons need similar deliverances to mine. (See My Deliverance from Confirmation, Infant Baptism, and Freemason Bondages, My Story chapter).

Park compares evil cults to Masonic-related orders. She said, "witches' covens and satanic cults are not much different from most mystical orders and brotherhoods, secretive sisterhoods, fraternities, sororities, all of whom are based on secret covenants. However, Satanists have no morality, self-discipline, or benevolent goals."[36]

Cast out the sins of secret orders listed above.

Many have believed that observing the biblical feasts is legalism. But I will show you that Easter, Christmas, and other holidays originate from witchcraft.

Yeshua's death saves us, his body broken, his blood shed, and his resurrection, not his birth.

> "For as often as you eat this bread and drink this cup, you proclaim the Lord's death till He comes. (1 Cor. 11:26)

There is no celebration of Yeshua's birth in the Bible after the angels, the shepherds, and wise men return to heaven, the fields, or their homes. Christmas trees are forbidden in Jeremiah 10:1-5.

> "Shall we continue in sin, that grace may abound?" (Rom. 6:1b)

Valentine's Day and Fornication

The Millers, deliverance ministers, said Valentine's Day is about fornication. "Keeping of dates and observances of these pagan practices opens the door of (one's) soul to the devil and idolatry."[37]

Carla Butaud, teaching for Lake Hamilton Bible Camp, said that sex (sin) is the highest form of witchcraft.[38]

CLF files indicate fornication brings in a master curse, the bastard curse named Krodeus. This person could not enter the congregation of the Lord for ten generations. (Deut. 23:2). With birth control or abortion, there may not be a baby, but the bastard spirit will still affect the whole family. (See Deliverance from Abortion, Birth Control. Appendix D).

Krodeus also comes in with Luciferina in infant baptism and freemasonry, with all sexual abuse and sexual sins, practicing witchcraft, and celebrating Halloween.[39] [40] Cast these all out.

The Sun God and his Festivals

Hislop said the Sun god represents the gods; Osiris, Baal, Baalim, and Molech.[41] He lists Christmas and Easter among five of Rome's innumerable festivals, which can be linked to Babylon.[42]

Ashteroth worship begins the spring Easter season of El Carnaval (the Mexican Mardi Gras) and completes it in Semana Santa.

Statues of huge bare-breasted mermaids were on the floats of El Carnaval (the Mexican Mardi Gras)! (See Siren, The Deliverance List for Familiar Spirits, Appendix G).

Unger indicates that Asherah, Asherat, the bare-breasted "Lady of the Sea," a consort of Baal, indulged in war and sex.[43]

My in-laws retired in an accursed town in Mexico where Indigenous tribes lead in Semana Santa (Holy Week) ceremonies held on beaches, where children are sacrificed.

Gorney said the beating of the drums begins three weeks before Semana Santa in Copper Canyon, Chihuahua, Mexico, with a mixture of Tarahumara and Catholic traditions. [44]

Good Friday and Easter Eve

Justus's Ritual calendar lists Good Friday, Easter Eve, the winter and summer solstices, the spring and fall equinoxes, one's birthday, any full moon, and nine more days: February 2, March 1, April 30, May 1, August 1, August 24, September 7, September 14, and October 31. Justus indicates the most important dates are April 30 and October 31. Justus support groups were formed to bring healing to those who survived intense Satanic ritual days, "days of unbelievable torture."[45] There are other days also.

There are three lunar witches' sabbaths: the full moon, the dark of the moon, and the new moon.

Elaine, the witch Dr. Rebecca Brown rescued, said men are crucified on the "Black Sabbath" before Easter![46]

January 6 Three King's Day, February 2, and October 31

On January 6, Three King's Day (El Día de Los Reyes Magos) there is a custom of serving a large ring of bread with a small figurine of a baby hidden inside. Whoever gets the piece with the baby is to invite people to a party on February 2.

February 2, El Dia de la Candelaria (Candlemas Day), is the day when babies are deliberately conceived with the intent of sacrificing them on Halloween.

December 21 to 25

Park described being involved in serious crimes before she was converted from witchcraft.[47]

She lists the eight Wiccan days of High Masses, including December 21 – 25. Park says, "many people are initiated into the worship of Satan these days."

Spiritual Warfare Against the Powers of Darkness

Park told us in the late 1980s, these days preceding the high days, "heats" are not getting longer but "hotter." She said Satan works very hard on Satanic holidays to kill, steal, and destroy believers' lives and faith. "Seven to ten days before each of the pagan high days, increase your spiritual warfare against the powers of darkness." But begin 13 days before Halloween. This author advises continuing until November 4 because of ceremonies in Mexico.[48]

I tried, to no avail, to get people at a church to do spiritual warfare before Halloween, 2020. I did the warfare, using lists from the CLF files, but I resisted the urge from Yeshua to war again on the eve of Halloween. Then I received an email that evening that the pastor's granddaughter whose parents are missionaries in Guatemala, had drowned mysteriously at a resort. This was a tragedy.

Satanic Ritual Abuse

Yeshua abhors the sacrifice of children, whether by deprivations of love, abandonment, divorce, molestation, abortion, methods of birth control, or actually killing them. See Semana Santa, chapter 7. These may bring hurricanes, strange floods, and water damage.

Yeshua said:

> "It would be better for him if a millstone were hung around his neck, and he were thrown into the sea, than that he should offend one of these little ones." (Matt. 18:6 NKJV).

Because King Manasseh sacrificed his son to Molech, God sent Judah into captivity for seventy years. (2 Kings 21:1,6; 2 Chron. 33:11–15).

Tom Horn created the movie "Silent Cry."[49] "Those that purchase children for sex slavery need you to believe it is all baseless conspiracy theories." "The horrors of child sex trafficking and Satanic ritual abuse continue because many of us won't believe it happens."[50]

Dr. Brown said, in Satanic abuse, the child is exposed to molestation, physical pain, and death. Often the child is forced to kill. Fear is implanted by threats of death to the child or their loved ones if they tell.[51]

She encourages the parent to pray for and deliver the child. She cautioned about going to the authorities because she believed, in 1987, all the agencies were infiltrated by Satanists, and the parent could lose their child.[52]

Dave Bryan wrote The Serpent and the Savior, telling a story about delivering Deborah Joy, Anton Levay's daughter, from the plans of her father to sacrifice her at Halloween. This ministry delivers out alter personalities, considering them to be demon spirits. (Bryan, See Instructions Regarding the Deliverances in This Book. Also see Jess Parker, References)

Climbing of The Devil's Tower Monument in Wyoming, USA, is discouraged in June because of "ceremonies." A friend said babies are thrown off the monument in these ceremonies.[53]

Cast out Nimrod, a spirit over Christmas trees, pyramids, and towers. (Gen. 10:8-10, 11:1-9).[54]

Cast out curses that came with the worship of Osiris, Baal, Astaroth, and Molech, because they are linked to sacrificing babies and children. (1 Kings 11:1-13; Jeremiah 32:35).

Cast out Molech, an angel of death, related to Buddha, also over abandonment by father.[55] (See Deliverance from Abortion, Birth Control, Appendix D).

What Does the Bible Say About Baptism?

Biblical baptism is not a substitute for trusting in the blood of Yeshua to wash our sins away. (1 Peter 1:16-19; Heb. 9:22). Nowhere in the Bible is immersion baptism used for deliverance.

Baptism must be preceded by repentance and believing in Yeshua. (Matt. 3:1-8; Mark 16:16).

It is immersion baptism. Many, including Yeshua were immersed by John in the Jordan river. (Matt. 3:5-17). It is wrong to baptize babies by sprinkling or immersion. They can't repent or believe.

Yeshua instructed to baptize in the name of the Father, Son, and Holy Spirit. (Matt. 28:19).

"Unless one is born of water and the Spirit, he cannot enter the kingdom of God." (John 3:5b NKJV).

"Unless one is born of water" (v. 5b) speaks of the baby swimming in the sack of amniotic fluid in the mother's womb before birth. The "water" does not refer to infant baptism. I use Hayes' "Developing Unborn Baby at 8 Weeks" to illustrate this.[56]

Goddesses Enter with Infant Baptism

Tom Horn documents that the church's sacraments (not just infant baptism) are sorcery.[57]

I became a spiritual sacrifice to Molech when I was baptized as a baby. The cross drawn on my brow and breast brought the curse of Molech and Tammuz. (See below). Crosses are about being cursed. (Gal 3:13). Yeshua took our curse. Pastors and priests should not be drawing crosses on babies or on the foreheads of adults with anointing oil. I told a woman who had left the Catholic Church to quit crossing herself.

In 2008, I learned that the "curse of Luciferina" comes into a person with oaths, in secret orders like infant baptism and the freemasons, bringing a curse on the person and their descendants."[58] (Exodus 20:1-6). Luciferina also lives in the churches where babies are baptized. This curse does not leave with a prayer for salvation or with immersion baptism. It must be renounced and delivered.

The CLF Luciferina deliverance pattern indicates the spirit of Mary comes in with infant baptism. The "a" on the end of Luciferina makes the name a feminine form, a goddess. The wife of Nimrod in the Lucifer trinity is Semiramis. She began crucifixion on crosses in remembrance of her son, Tammuz.[59] Cast out the goddesses under Luciferina; Mary, Isis under Osiris, and Semiramis under Nimrod. Woodrow adds Diana (under Zeus) and Astarte (Astaroth) (under Baal). [60]

(See Six-pointed Star, Symbols and Emblems that Bring Curses chapter). (See Names of Demons in the New Testament, Teaching on Actual Deliverance chapter).

CLF files indicate the curse of Luciferina brings a second curse spirit, Krodeus. (See Valentine's Day and Fornication).

Krodeus accounts for the reported molestation of children in churches and Boy, Girl, and Cub Scouts troops. Renounce, forgive, and cast out all spirits over infant, child, teen, or adult sexual abuse, sexual addiction, or pedophilia in all generations of your family. Do not confront perpetrators without professional or legal help. (See Luther, Deliverance from Curses chapter).

Like myself and my mother, girls and women may not hear warnings about boys and men. Deliver out the spirits of Krodeus and Isis.

There is a common false doctrine, even in print, that God allows the molestation of children. These authors are worshiping the wrong God! Matthew 18:6 proves this doctrine to be a lie. Parents who are not delivered from their own sexual abuse, churches and organizations that cover up the reports of the rapes, and judges who do not sentence pedophiles to prison, allow this molestation. (See Threats of Ex-communication, Deliverance from Traumas chapter. See Appendix J).

Two Principalities, Put Satanachia and Nebiros, also enter with infant baptism. (See 80-list, Appendix E).

Infant baptism brings in Zombie, and Zeus curses

Two inherited curse spirits come in with infant baptism and witchcraft initiations through the last name; Zombie is the passive failure spirit, and Zeus is the dominant achieving spirit.[61]

A Zombie/Zeus and Fear Deliverance Pattern, abbreviated

Cast these out.

Overwhelming fears: Fear of facing self. Fear of just being.

Overwhelming, inherited fears: Inability to give and receive love—inability to receive the blessings of Yahveh (God).

A suppressed and paralyzed will. Acting out, mechanically doing what they tell you to do.

These spirits block emotions and bring false peace, horror, and false submission (to authorities).

Zombies come in through death of some kind and suppress the will (even the will to live).[62]

Landry says that a child copes by becoming passive in a harrowing situation, pretending to agree to the (abuse) to survive. The child assumes they have caused or are guilty of the (abuse) by an authority figure. As an adult in deliverance counseling, this person will pretend to agree with the deliverance worker, but Landry says that this passivity allows nothing to happen in the deliverance session.[63]

Spiritual Death

Anna identified Zombies, Sargatanas, and Osiris over spiritual death.[64] These can be inherited so that a child is born spiritually dead. There is not just the need to be born again, described in John 3:7, but a need to be delivered from these curses over spiritual death that makes a person resistant to receiving eternal life. I prayed for an older man having chest pain who had been extremely resistant to salvation. Yeshua showed me he had a Zombie spirit of death from infant baptism. (See Death Spirits, Appendix K).

In 1959, my mother's uncle, J. O. Gisselquist, a Lutheran evangelist, agreed with Rev. Hallesby, saying that if a person was baptized as a baby, it is harder for him to convert when he sees himself as a sinner than if he had gone out and lived a life of sin.[65] We heard Gisselquist speak at the family Bible camp.

Another Lutheran Church evangelist, Herbert Mjorud, said when he would return to a Lutheran church a year after a great revival had occurred, "it appeared that nothing had ever happened."[66] A classmate at the Lutheran boarding school said she had gotten saved when Mjorud ministered in a country church. She was one of the few from our school who left the Lutheran church.

In 2014 and 2019, I returned to an annual reunion in a small town where my father had been a pastor for seven years and found few people who were really saved or even wanted to be saved. In contrast, I found three-fourths of the people who attended the July 2019 Lutheran boarding school reunion to be sure of eternal life.

In 2019, in the small town, one woman who had already left the Lutheran church renounced her infant baptism. Her brother had offended our family, and I insisted that he repent. His wife said yes to the Savior.

The Worship of Mary and Religious Leaders

We are to worship only the Father, Son, and Holy Spirit; Apostle Paul quotes Moses from Deuteronomy (D'Varim) 18:18-22. God told Moses he will raise a prophet *"like unto thee."*

> *"And it shall come to pass, that every soul, which will not hear that prophet, shall be destroyed from among the people."* (Acts 3:22-23)

Become a witness, a missionary where you are, and pray people will accept their Jewish Messiah.

We are not to worship religious leaders. Apostle Paul condemns this sin.

> *"They worshiped and served the creature, more than the Creator."* (Rom. 1:25).

(Also see Exodus (Sh'mot) 20:1-6.)

Even if the person you worshiped is deceased, cast their spirit out by their name, in the name of Yeshua. (Use The Deliverance List for Familiar Spirits, Appendix G).

We are not to pray to the dead, which is necromancy. (Deut. 18:9-14). Though Mary is alive in heaven, she can't hear our prayers. One woman at a laundromat said Mary would appear to her at a particular chapel; it was a demon pretending to be Mary.

Woodrow says the Catholic Church teaches that Mary is greater than Jesus.[67] Mary and Joseph had sons and daughters after Yeshua was born. (Matt. 1:24-25; 12:46-47; 13:55; Mk. 6:2-3).

The sister of Moses was named Meriam. The mother of Yeshua was a Jewish woman named Meriam, not Mary.

> *"Miriam, from whom was born Yeshua who is called the Messiah."* (Matt. 1:16 TLV)

Chick portrays Mary and the Masonic Isis, both with halos, standing on globes, with snakes under their feet.[68]

The Jesuit symbol, I H S

Chick and Hislop say the I H S represents the Egyptian trinity, Isis, Horus, & Seb.[69] "The mother, the child, and the father."[70] This Isis bears no connection to ISIS, the Islamic State terrorist group.

The I H S symbolized the Catholic Jesuit Order, Society of Jesus, founded in 1540.[71] Alberto Rivera, a former Jesuit Priest, confessed he took an oath to "make and wage relentless war, secretly or openly, against all heretics, protestants, and liberals, as I am directed to do." [72]If the communion wafer has the I H S on it, don't eat it. If it is plain and round, break it before you eat it. Hislop said it represents the sun god. Halley verified Rivera's claims and said the Jesuit's object was to recover territory lost to the Protestants and Mohammedans.[73]

Our Lutheran church had the I H S on the altar cloth. We had Mary, Isis, the Freemason and Egyptian goddess, and a Jesuit Catholic symbol in our church, and we didn't know it!

Why is the church enslaved to Egypt? Moses told the Israelites; that if they disobeyed, they would come under a curse. They would return to Egypt as enslaved people, but no one would buy them. (Deut. 28:68).

This author believes the Jesuit trinity of the I H S enters priests and pastors at their ordination and into youth at confirmation. But some persons are trained as Jesuits. Cast out the spirit of the Jesuits that could cause you to oppose the gospel or because the Jesuits may have persecuted you.

One day this prophecy will be fulfilled; "Babylon the great is fallen." (Rev. 18:2).

(See More on the Jesuits, Appendix I).

The Worship of Freemason gods

Deliver these out.

Campbell said the layout of the Washington DC Federal Center, designed by a Mason appointed by George Washington, is like a coffin.[74] There is a statue of Isis in the Masonic temple in Washington DC. He names other gods of Freemasonry; Osiris, Baal, Bacchus, and the Great Architect of the Universe (Lucifer). He expressed concern that our nation's government may have been symbolically offered to the kingdom of darkness through Masonic rituals.[75]

Anna documents that the goddess Isis is over secrecy. Stevens said the blood red rose symbolizes Freemasonry's secrecy and silence. [76]

Isis, over secrecy, can cause the memory of trauma to be blocked out or repressed, causing depression. (See Sargatanas, 80-list, Appendix E).

Freemason-related organizations are brotherhoods, lodges, and fraternal organizations; like Scouting, the Mormon church, fraternities, sororities, the Independent Order of Foresters (a fraternal organization), and the Jaycees. Selwyn Stevens has a complete list in *Unmasking Freemasonry*.

Kitchen said in the seventeenth degree of Freemasonry, the demon Abaddon (Rev. 9:11) is worshiped. The initiate cuts his arm, bleeds into a bowl, and throws his blood onto the altar. He takes his oath on the New Testament in the eighteenth degree and then burns it! Break the curse of "being emotionally and physically ravaged all your life." I believe Osiris is one spirit over this. Cast out the witchcraft of the Kabbala and Rosicrucianism, secrecy, silence, and spirits of death. Cast out not being able to read the New Testament. [77]

Stevens says Grand Orient Freemason Lodges found in Catholic countries are most occultic and atheistic. [78]

The Ancient Arabic Order of the Mystic Shrine of Freemasonry, the 33rd degree, worships Allah as the "god of their fathers."[79] These men oppose the gospel and the nation of Israel.

Pastor Eloyse identified the trinities of Lucifer and Satan. Stevens identified Hindu, Egyptian, and Druid Freemason trinities in specific degrees of Freemasonry initiations.[80]

The 24th-degree Egyptian gods; Osiris, Isis, and Horus.

The 26th-degree Druid gods; Odin, Frea, and Thor. Druid gods have come from England, Scandinavia, and Germany. This cult is prevalent and most visible at Halloween.

The 32nd degree, Hindu gods: Brahma, creator; Vishnu, preserver; and Shiva, destroyer. Pastor Eloyse knew Shiva to be Put Satanachia. (See 80-list, Appendix E).

Hindu gods are evident in Eastern religion, New Age spiritualism, alternative medicines, acupuncture, relaxation response, guided imagery, biofeedback, essential oils, Yoga, Tai chi, Martial arts, cremation, and more. The relaxation response was part of my father's cardiac rehabilitation class and a women's healing seminar in a church sanctuary! The mentally ill, the developmentally disabled, children, the elderly, and people desperate for healing, all vulnerable, are participating in these activities.

A minister from India, Sukhwant Bhatia, formerly of the Sikh religion, said the Catholic Church they see portrayed in movies made in the USA resembles Hinduism.[81][82]

Park adds the sun god Ra and Satan-Lucifer, saying these Freemason initiations are nearly identical to those used by witchcraft.[83]

Cast out the above trinities who, as John 10:10 says, are come "to steel, and to kill, and to destroy." Cast out freemasonry over our government and our money. (See Symbols and Emblems That Bring Curses chapter.) Cast out the antichrist spirit of Bacchus over wine and other alcohol used in these organizations. (See Freemasonry, References).

> "Woe unto them that rise up early in the morning, that they may follow strong drink; that continue until night, till wine inflame them!" (Is. 5:11).

The Military of the USA is under Freemasonry

Cast out the curses men in the military receive because they are serving under the United States, under Freemasonry's bondage. Cast out the curse of Nimrod from being yelled at and verbally cursed by your drill sergeant while going through basic training. Repent for committing gross sins, viewing pornography, fornication, conceiving bastard children, and using drugs and alcohol.

Lopez documents that persons in the military are getting PTSD for two reasons. Cast out the curse that comes with the trauma of sexual abuse at their assigned post and having been traumatized from being in a war zone.[84] The military provides resources for both types of traumas.

In late 1989, Point Man Ministries headquarters reported that Buddhist priests had cursed American troops during the Vietnam war.[85] Cast out voodoo and witchcraft curses that have been placed on all of the military, not just those in a war zone. Cast out poverty, wandering, lack of peace, and divorce; curses that were placed on you.

Davis lists many more curses to cast out and blesses you with "God's steps to recovery from the PTSD Curse." This is an excellent prayer for deliverance.[86] I suggest going through it frequently. (Also, see the Deliverance List for Familiar Spirits, Appendix G).

These curses are real. My first husband and all my eight brothers and brothers-in-law who have been in the military have had at least one divorce or separation.

The husband is cautioned about dealing treacherously against his "wife by covenant" because Yah "seeks godly offspring." (Mal. 2:13-17).

A man teaching the Torah at Beit Tikvah said his wife asked him for a separation when their son was suffering acutely from a schizoaffective disorder because he sought to pray for his son's deliverance. His attorney wrote a more generous separation agreement than her attorney. By God's grace, the marriage was restored in eleven months. He refers to Jacob's continual support of Leah, the less loved wife, and Yeshua's and Apostle Paul's advocacy for marriage. (Gen. 29:30, 30:20-21; Matthew 19:1-10; 1 Cor. 7:10-11).

Worship of the Gods of Indigenous Peoples

Sanchez said communities of Sephardic Jews were separated during the Inquisition in the New World, forcing them to intermarry with the indigenous peoples, becoming genetically and spiritually mixed with the Indigenous peoples. A great uncle on my father's side was taken captive by American Indians during the Civil War. Many other races have intermarried with these peoples or unknowingly have this ancestry.

We are forbidden to worship Molech, practice divination, be an observer of times, an enchanter, a witch, a charmer, a consulter with familiar spirits, a wizard, or a necromancer. (Deut. 18:9-12).

In the summer of 2020, I wrote eighty pages on the Boy Scouts. There are hundreds of Boy Scout camps worldwide, in Israel, in Mexico. All who participate in Boy or Girl Scouting, their ceremonies, and handicrafts, take in the spirits of these American Indians and other indigenous tribes. My father was inducted into the Boy Scout Order of the Arrow at a Scout camp in North Dakota in 1959. My husband, at a camp south of Mexico City in 1972, when his family lived in Mexico.

Park, half American Indian, wrote in "Witchcraft Idolatry and Indian Ways," "all the worship unto images, idols, and spirits is heathenism and paganism. The rituals and ceremonies are unto beasts, animals, fowls, harvests, stars, demon spirits, and spirit guides. The spirit guides (familiar spirits or fallen angels) work the spirit of divination and send forth agents (lesser entities) often considered deities, that pose as gods or goddesses."[87]

Park commands to destroy all accursed things used in this demon spirit worship. Clothing, masks, moccasins, rattles, feathers, grains, parts or designs of beasts, fowl, fish, and creeping things. Also, the Ojo de Dios (God's eye), American Indian dolls, blankets, rugs, and jewelry, especially silver and turquoise.[88] This author adds the medicine wheel or dream catcher and advises you to cease visiting their pow-wows, museums, cemeteries, reservations, caves, and monuments.

Park said that participation in the worship of chants, prayers, dances, or ceremonial rituals that have come down through the teachings from generation to generation or acquiring these articles, or those with pagan symbols, has brought a curse on people and their families. Renounce every ancestral spirit, spirit guide, and demon spirit. Repent and apply the blood of Jesus between you and the spirits.[89] (Deut. 7:26; Acts 19:19).

Cast out the above, especially the curses from you or your ancestors having sacrificed to, or being the sacrifice to, the god, Molech; the terrors, hate, destruction, and spirits of death. If you minister to or with these people, Hispanics or Scouts, get deliverance from these spirits of the indigenous tribes as well as their other bondages. (For more spirits to cast out, see Appendices A, L & M. See Satanic Ritual Abuse, Have no other Gods chapter).

Witchcraft from Africa in the Church Music

The worship of Orisha gods is African witchcraft, brought with those forced to serve as enslaved people in the southern United States of America. Landry said the Orisha drums, gourd rattles, and dance are brought into the church worship music, bringing generational curses and demon possession instead of the true Holy Spirit.[90] The music was wild one Sunday, so I went into the large church foyer. The man who was a greeter was dancing with a woman who wasn't his wife! Orisha music and dance, including Macumba, have also come into the church through recent African refugees. African ancestry may have also brought bondages of Catholicism, Orthodoxy, Freemasonry, and Islam.

8

Symbols and Emblems that Bring Curses

Only the seven-branch menorah was used as a symbol in the tabernacle. All Freemasonry, Scouting, and witchcraft symbols bring curses; Kitchen, Stevens, and Park have exposed many of these symbols.

People are *"perishing for lack of knowledge."* (Hos. 4:6).

Park said people have been under the persuasion and influence of demonic powers for generations by having these emblems in their homes or possession. She faults many symbols, including the six-pointed star, three of the five-pointed stars, the pyramid and the eye on the back of the US dollar, and the Ankh cross.[91] She says the asterisk and stars, symbols for hexes, are used for buttons on moccasins and boots.[92] Walmart uses the asterisk symbol. Selwyn Stevens faults the Freemason symbol of the Point within a Circle from pagan phallus worship, which seems to be the symbol of the Target store. (See more symbols in: The Worship of Gods of Indigenous Peoples, Have no Other God's chapter).

> Isaiah said, *"the Lord of Hosts (shall) come down to fight for Mount Zion, ... in that day every man shall cast away his idols of silver, and his idols of gold, which your own hands have made unto you for a sin."* (Is. 31:4b, 7)

Flags hanging in many churches have the sun, the moon, or stars on them, which are prohibited in Exodus 20:3-5. Statues are also prohibited.

A Hispanic pastor had meetings at a food bank on West Colfax. He put a sign on the door. If Jesus was killed with a gun, would you wear a gun around your neck?

Alberto Rivera said the crucifix is a Jesuit symbol for vengeance and death. [93]

The Six-Pointed Star

Starting with Chanukah in December 2007, I received attacks after attending four meetings where the six-pointed star was displayed. This caused me to investigate this symbol. In Acts 7:42-43, Stephen quotes Amos and connects this star to Molech and going into captivity. (Molech, See Satanic Ritual Abuse, Have No Other Gods chapter.)

In a lesson on Tammuz in 1979, Pastor Eloyse identified the six powerful entities on the six-pointed star. The 80-list helped her recognize the three points of the downward pointing triangle, representing the trinity under Satan; Baal or Beelzebub, Ashtaroth, and Put Satanachia. (See The 80-list, Appendix E).

She taught, the three points of the upward pointing triangle represent Lucifer; Nimrod, Semiramis, and Tammuz.[94] According to her, this star is under Python.[95]

Bible verses on Lucifer, (Is. 14:12-21 only KJV, NKJV). Nimrod, (Gen. 10:8-10). Tammuz, (Ezek. 8:14).

According to Park, this star is used in blood sacrifices and magic, "the conjuring of forces to hypnotize and seduce." "Evil spirits gather in force at the summons of the person working the 'hex.'" [96]

This star is having detrimental effects on persons attending congregations. Two of these congregations brought more troubles by displaying two stars. I know of three women who left the Messianic because of the way women were treated at one of these congregations. I know three Messianic persons including a leader who have gone to Rabbinic Judaism. I encountered three persons who had been Messianic from childhood. A woman who had a Bat Mitzvah had gone to Buddhism. A professional person was not sure of going to heaven. A young man on the RTD bus asked if they knew I was witnessing. I made him take Sid Roth's Book, *They Thought for Themselves*, stories of ten Jewish persons who believe in the Messiah.

Pastor Eloyse said Put Satanachia, one of the six demonic powers on this star, is over false doctrines. One leader who had two stars said it is "salvation by works" to not take the mark of the beast! (See Concerns about Messianic Judaism, The Biblical Feasts and Sabbaths chapter).

Graham, a Messianic leader who wrote *The Six-Pointed Star*, was challenged by an Orthodox Jew about using this symbol. Graham found this star has no Jewish origin but was popularized by Rothschild, used by Hitler against the Jews, and then on the flag of Israel. It is used in witchcraft and the Cabala.[97]

In the 4th edition of his book, he connects King Solomon and this star to Freemasonry and the Anti-Christ. (Amos 5:26; Dan. 8:24-27). [98]

Yvonne Kitchen's book on Freemasonry delineates so many similarities, but blasphemies to Solomon's temple in Jerusalem that I believe the next Temple built will be a Freemasonry temple of the Anti-Messiah. Ron Cantor, a Messianic Rabbi in Israel, agrees, citing Daniel 9:27. He said we should look for the fourth temple, not the third. (See References).

9

Teaching on Actual Deliverance

There are four commands for waring against demons: bind (Matt.16:19), rebuke (Jude 9), take authority over (Luke 9:1), and cast out.

"*And these signs shall follow them that believe; In my name shall they cast out devils.*" Demons. (NKJV) (Mark 16:17a).

As I deliver myself or others, I say, "Go, in the name of Yeshua." The demon frequently says, "I'm not in here. I'm not going to leave." I abbreviate and record this "INIH, INGTL." Then I may get my deliverance or a proxy deliverance for the other person.

A yawn, cough, or a burp, sometimes vomiting, are signs of deliverance. I record the type of deliverance that I receive. (Mark 1:25-26 ; 9:25-27; 16:20; Acts 2:43, 8:5-8). I record my deliverances and file them to use for subsequent deliverance. This was beneficial the second time I got COVID-19, because I knew what to cast out and how to gain strength afterward. (See Deliverance from Curses chapter).

In Mark 9:29, Yeshua said fasting and prayer are necessary to deliver strong demons. These demons must also be cast out.

Anna would call out spirits in four ways: inherited, active, repressed, and dormant. I added "transferred." Abuse from childhood can be transferred onto relationships later in life, blocking love. (Rom. 5:12). Pastor Eloyse said false blame and hate could be transferred onto mothers. This Satanic Transference can hinder their effectiveness in the home.[99] (See Hatred of Women and Children, Deliverance from Traumas chapter).

Deliverance can take place in individual or group sessions. In Body ministry, several persons minister to one person. Individual deliverances were recorded and filed. Pastor Eloyse and her workers delivered out demons by their names, by the grounds (how they came in), by their works, addictions, and more characteristics. Pastor Eloyse compiled and called these "demon patterns." She believed the demons were not just in the soul or oppressing from the outside, but in the spirit, even though the person may have the Holy Spirit. (2 Cor. 7:1). The Holy Spirit reveals what we need deliverance from.

People with religious spirits will not accept deliverance. Remit their sins and possibly proxy deliverances for them. Pastor Eloyse ministered to those who were desperate.

These demons can be sent to the bottom of the deepest sea, KJV, or the abyss, NKJV. (Luke 8:31).

Casting out Demons by Proper Names

Exodus 20:3-5, and Joshua 23:6-8, prohibit us from having, making, bowing down to, serving, naming, or swearing by other gods. Both curses and demon gods have names that may be used in teaching deliverance and delivering out the demons.

Pastor Eloyse said, "If the demon is cast out by its name, the authority and power of the demon is gone. "In intercessory deliverance, for someone who is not present, the use of the names of demons releases the persons to seek help. She knew Satan attacks deliverance ministries that use proper names. He does not want success in the deliverance."[100] Most Christians are afraid of demons and persons who minister deliverance and do spiritual warfare. Satan wants deliverance ministries maligned by others, and opposing one another, so few persons in bondage are set free. (Luke 9:49-50).

Casting out demons by their names is a higher level of deliverance. The Holy Spirit revealed these names of demons to Pastor Eloyse to set people free. (Is. 61:1). I learned to use the names of demons in deliverance and spiritual warfare at CLF. Yeshua uses women to minister deliverance.

"And base things of the world, and things which are despised, hath God has chosen, yea, and things which are not, to bring to not things that are." (1 Cor. 1:28).

Pastor Eloyse's use of the names of demons from the 80-list accomplished a miracle deliverance of a woman she had not previously been able to deliver. She found that one principality at a time could be delivered when working to deliver a dedicated believer. But it may take more than one deliverance session.

I have used the 80-list, Pastor Eloyse's list of Sexual Lust Demons and many other CLF lists for deliverance and spiritual warfare. (See App. E, F, & N). (See Addendum II, Spiritual Warfare).

The authors I have referenced, Campbell, Kitchen, Stevens, and Hislop, have exposed the names of demons. Unger describes and names forty-one demon gods and goddesses from the Bible.[101]

Names of Demons in the New Testament

There was a demon-possessed man in the country of the Gadarenes.

> "Jesus asked him, saying, "What is your name? And he said, "Legion," because many demons had entered him."
> (Luke 8:30 NKJV)

People who hated Yeshua's miracles accused him of casting out demons using the power of a demon named Beelzebub.

Yeshua's response indicates that he could not use both Satan and the Holy Spirit's power to cast out demons. (Luke 11:14-20). (Beelzebub, See The 80-list, Appendix E).

> "But if I cast out demons with the finger of God, surely the kingdom of God has come upon you." (Luke 11:20 NKJV).

Jupiter and Mercurius are Roman gods. (Acts 14:12 KJV). Zeus and Hermes are Greek gods named in the NKJV.

The temple of Diana was in Ephesus. It was believed she fell from Zeus. (Acts 19:23-41).

Can a Christian Have a Demon?

Yeshua was the Messiah. He fulfilled Isaiah 61:1, coming to set the captives free, delivering many persons, including a daughter of Abraham on the sabbath day. (Luke 13:16) (See also Luke 4:18, 8:1-3).

Some religious leaders won't admit a Christian can have a demon. They usually say a person is not really saved if they can't stop sinning and if they need deliverance. This doctrine keeps people in churches silent about some problems instead of requesting prayer and deliverance.

Cheryl Bryan, at the Isaiah 61 Conference, said regarding Deborah Joy's deliverance, Abba's heart adores humanity amidst their struggle. The church adores humanity when they are good. (Bryan, see References).

I accepted the Savior in 1961 and 1983. I needed deliverance from demons and curses, even after I left the sin and victimization of Nebraska in 1983. I took a psychological test in 1996 that indicated I was not "mentally ill," but I received great deliverances from Anna in 1999. I am still delivering myself and receiving deliverance counseling.

On Wednesday evenings, the assistant pastor at a Foursquare church led a recurrent discussion, "Can a Christian have a Demon?" Some women in the group believed a Christian could have a Demon. This topic irritated me, so I began going to

Eda and Hector's church on Wednesday.[102] Returning with my husband and finding the same topic repeated, I spoke to him after the lesson, saying I wanted him to be sure he was going to heaven. He said that was a private matter. I was shocked! He is not sure about going to heaven.

Whetstone, now a world minister, passed all of the psychological tests, but his mother said he had demons.[103] Churches put literature in the women's restroom for those who are being abused or who need healing after abortions.

Many teens in a church told Lisa Bevere they had been sexually violated and molested at the hands of those they'd trusted. [104]

A former "medicine man" in the Boy Scout Order of the Arrow initiation revealed that he was to call up spirits from the woods, determine their names, and give them as spirit guides to the other members. This caused him, a believer, severe oppression and hindrances, but after deliverance by Bell, he was able to fulfill his ministry in France. [105]

Unger wrote, What Demons Can Do to Saints. (See References).

Pastor Eloyse and Anna documented the names of many demons that cause illnesses.[106] Taylor said the eighty spirits on his list could take over the human body. (See The 80-list, Appendix E).

The many deliverance ministries worldwide indicate that Christians seek and receive deliverance.

Mediums, Familiar Spirits, and Secret Orders

On an undated pink note page, I wrote: Pastor Eloyse and Anna knew that mediums, familiar spirits, and secret orders do not come out with a prayer of salvation or immersion baptism.

A Medium

Pastor Eloyse believed mediums were channels for curses from previous generations.[107] (Lev. 19:31 NKJV, Is. 8:19 NKJV).

Irene Park compared a medium to a warlock, wizard, and witch.[108]

Yvonne Kitchen said, "A Master Mason (of the third degree of freemasonry) is a medium through which demons can speak." [109]

> *"(King) Josiah put away those who consulted mediums and spiritists, that he might perform the words of the law which were written in the book that Hilkiah the priest found in the house of the Lord."* (2 Kings 23:24 NKJV)

The King James Version uses "familiar spirits," not mediums.

Familiar Spirits

Familiar spirits come through sex sins, molestation, or frequent kissing. Familiar spirits can also come through abuse, idolatry, religious leadership, or any close relationship like teachers, medical professionals, and the media. Cast out every aspect of sin or trauma. (See Deliverance List for Familiar Spirits, Appendix G).

Meridel Rawlings wrote of Pastor Eloyse's biblical knowledge and spiritual skill, used under the authority of the Almighty God to define and deliver her from criminal minds that locked her in the prison of incest.

Having been traumatized by her grandfather, who was a pastor, her father (who repented), and her uncle, Rawlings said, "I called out their names (familiar spirits) and demanded in the Name of the Living God that the "evil will" of each one leave my life."[110] Her Doctoral theses examined families of incest from four different faiths.

10

Deliverance from Curses

Gene and Erline Moody, authors of many deliverance books, said, "If the demons have a right to remain before God due to a curse, you will not be able to cast them out. If you cast them out, they will come back in." But they quote Joel.

> *"For I will cleanse their blood that I have not cleansed, for the Lord dwelleth in Zion."* (Joel 3:21)[111]

I believe the psychiatric term, "Fixed Delusions," are lies people believe. They are difficult to root out because curses reinforce these lies.

Some believe that Yeshua erased all curses on the cross, but curses will exist until Satan is thrown into the lake of fire and the throne of the Lamb and God, the Father, is established. Then there will be no more curses. (Gal. 3:13; Rev. 20:10; Rev. 22:3).

Brawner, who left her profession as a medical doctor to minister the gospel, said, Jesus bore our curse on the cross. Still, it is only an actual experience for us to be healed and free in the "ordeal of childbirth" if this healing is "believed and appropriated." (Gal. 3:13).[112]

How Curses Enter

> *Moses said, "if thou wilt not hearken unto the voice of the Lord thy God, to observe to do all his commandments*

and his statutes which I command thee this day; that all these curses shall come upon thee, and overtake thee." (Deut., D'Varim, 28:15 NKJV).

The Difference Between Spells and Curses

Park said spells are cast on humans, fowl, or animals. Then the minds of demons work to change the personality, features, or actions of the being by divination, to manipulate, attack or kill (such as with illnesses).

A curse and hexes can bring destruction for three, four, or ten generations. (Ex. 20:3-5, Deut. 23:2). In addition to humans, fowl, and animals, a curse can be cast on inanimate objects like jewelry, statues, masks, and souvenirs with carvings, paintings, or designs. The spirit of divination divines through the object. Curses (like Luther or Luciferina) can remain in a building or bring in a noisy poltergeist.[113]

Park said witches pray for the "mangling of bodies." They also send spells on government leaders, pastors, missionaries, those who believe in Yeshua, and their families. Accidents, deaths, and illnesses are more prevalent on witches' sabbaths.

Anyone can send spells. Fernando Perez alerts us to stand against every evil force motivated by jealousy, hate, envy, and revenge. (Perez, see References).

Cast out Enyo and Oblivio, a death wish, over all curses.[114] Choose life and blessings. (Deut. 30:19). (See App. K). (See Addendum II, The Tithe Broke the Spell)

What Curses Do to You

The results of curses are listed in Deuteronomy, D'Varim, 28:16-68. If believers had no curses today, they would have none of the problems Moses speaks of.

Accidents, early deaths, loss of wife and children, rejection, destruction, war, drought, madness, victimization, being scattered among other nations, and serving their gods. Fear, terror, and anguish make you worthless, even as enslaved people. No one will hire you.

If we don't obey Yah, Father God, serving him with joy when we have abundance, we will serve our enemies with lack. (Deut. 28:46-48).

You can identify people who have curses in several ways. They have serious illnesses, lack assurance of eternal life, and cannot work for Yeshua. Curses created the wretched, miserable, poor, blind, and naked, end-times church of Laodicea. (Rev. 3:17). Curses create unbelief and hatred of God and take many to hell, which was never intended for people. (Matt. 25:41). Hell, and destruction awaits the unbeliever. (Mark 16:16b; Acts 3:22-23).

Many people who have had infant baptism or have belonged to freemason-related organizations and those who have had traumas may not be sure of going to heaven, even after confessing their sins. I have learned to even ask pastors if they are confident about going to heaven.

Dr. Rebecca Brown wrote, *Unbroken Curses: Hidden Source of Trouble in the Christian's Life*. (See References). In chapter 13 of *He Came to set the Captives Free*, Brown says any dealings with Satan are "Doorways" for curses.

A man with a severe heart attack believed he was going to hell because a Voodoo curse had been placed on him fifty years earlier, preventing him from accepting Jesus. Brown, out loud, bound Satan and his demons in the name of Jesus, freeing him to accept Jesus and receive peace before he died.

Curses over Families and Nations

Kitchen said, "curses stop whole families from going on with God." For generations, curses can affect a family, whole communities, tribes, and nations. Each degree of Freemasonry brings curses to specific parts of the body. Examine your family tree for early deaths and the type of death to identify a curse over your family line.[115]

Families and deliverance ministries should discern if there are curses that need to be broken. In my mother's family, the older generations were led by Lutheran pastors and seminary presidents. My father, a Lutheran pastor, led two boy scout troops. My first husband's families were Nazarene pastors and, like himself, church musicians, but he joined the military and the Jaycees. I was a girl scout leader, and our children were in Scouting.

This brought more curses and sin, a rare disease for my mother, disabilities, divorces, early deaths, cancer, bladder leaks, and other illnesses, including child and adult sexual abuse, addictions, spiritual problems, and unbelief. Curses caused some to remain single or marry the wrong person. Birth control caused some to have few or no children. A nephew is a transsexual because he was separated from his father when his parents divorced, and a Boy Scout leader raped him. He refused to file a claim of sexual abuse against the bankruptcy court for the Boy Scouts of America by the November 16, 2020 deadline. In my second husband's family, freemasonry and unbelief were stronger, and four of five had cancer

Lucario said, "complex trauma survivors often endure a loss of faith. This can be about people, the world as good, religion, and a loss of faith about self."[116] All of my family left the Lutheran church but my parents had to return to keep their benefits. Some of us got the Holy Spirit with tongues. I began keeping the feasts and sabbaths and using the name Yeshua. (See Lucario, Appendix H).

COVID-19

Curses bring pestilences that will cleave to you. (Deut. 28:21-22). Fever. Chronic illnesses or permanent disabilities. The world and the church have been traumatized by the Pandemic. (Matt. 24:8-14). I believe witchcraft spells have been assigned to pastors causing many to die from COVID-19. When I was in ICU with COVID-19 pneumonia in 2020, Yeshua gave me over thirty bondages to cast out.

At least three were curses from the 1960s. In both 2020 and 2022, Oblivio and Zombie spirits preceded the witchcraft curse of the virus. Beelzebub and Baphomet brought isolation that didn't want to leave me. I had to again battle the spirit guide of Luther, and homosexual spirits that brought irritability against my husband the day before I got a negative COVID-19 test in 2022. Along with COVID-19, transsexuality has been rising. COVID-19 deliverance is on my website, as well as songs I sang in a nursing home before COVID-19.[117]

How to Remove Curses

Never send a curse back to where it originated. This is witchcraft. You are to bless the sender, and you want them to get saved. (Luke 6:28). You may have to distance yourself from them.

Forgive your ancestors and those of your spouse, even if they are deceased. (Gen. 2:24). Forgive and remit their sins if they are living—Minister freedom by prayer walking, spiritual warfare, and proxy deliverance. (See Remitting Sins Chapter).

Deliver out the "grounds" for the curse: inherited or personal, from secret orders, sins, sexual relationships, or traumas. (See Perez, above).

Deliver out the results of the curses: early death, illnesses, addictions, disabilities, poverty, divorce, or separations. (See, "What Curses Do to You," above.)

Deliver out the Deliverance List for Familiar Spirits, Appendix G. If you are spiritually strong, deliver the nine major principalities on the 80-list. Deliver out the curses I have included in this book.

(See Addendum II, Krodeus, the Bastard Curse).

Get deliverances; Brother Carlos and Fernando Perez on YouTube. Mark Hemans, Zoom. Order Whetstone's or Brown's books on curses in Spanish or English, Prince's in English only. (See References).

More Curses and Demons to Cast Out

All names of demons in this section are from CLF deliverance files unless otherwise identified. Remember to bind Baal and Beelzebub. Then cast these all out.

- Cast out "being the cursed one."
- The hatred of God and people is extreme in witchcraft. Especially hatred of those who believe in Yeshua. Hatred is like murder. (1 John 3:15).
- Hatred comes from mixing the gospel in either the Sunday or Sabbath church with witchcraft.
- Lucifer, Sabean, and Put Satanachia are over hatred.[118] Lucifer kills his own people and destroys his own land. (Is. 14:20).
- Nimrod, under Lucifer, is the curse that comes from cursing and being cursed or yelled at.[119]
- Nimrod is over non-communication, sadism, and a wall of hate between self and others.[120]
- Lust is really hatred. Sabean, in Ezekiel chapter 23, especially verses 39 and 42, shows the connection between lust and sacrifice of children among those who pretended to worship Yahveh.[121]
- The demon spirit of Sytry "produces nudity." (See 80-list, Appendix E). Voyeurism and exhibitionism can come from having been molested. Anna said that the curse is on the one who looks.

The Curse of Antisemitism

Rejection of the biblical feasts, the sabbaths, and the name Yeshua, is antisemitic. Johnson reports that centuries of Catholic and Lutheran antisemitism culminated in Hitlerism. Germany is still paying survivors of the Holocaust, giving them a dollar for each day they were imprisoned, forced to live in a ghetto, or wear a star.[122]

Luther, A Demon of Antisemitism and Abuse over the Protestant Church

I saw a demon in my father's basement office, which doubled as a bedroom, on November 7, 2002. My husband was hitting me in bed, which he never did. I woke up, saw the see-through warty demon on him, and said, "Go!" Anna and I later discerned this spirit's names are Luther and nudity. CLF learned that all the names of demons that begin with "Lu" are under Lucifer.

Anna said Luther is over an inherited family pattern of abuse which resides in many Protestant persons, families, homes, and churches. Cast out the demonic trinity, the family or familiar spirit of "Luther," your last name, and Put Satanachia. Luther is a slave driver, a controller, and a saboteur, over nudity, incest, and child molestations, even at Bible camps. (Put Satanachia, see the 80-list, Appendix E, and see Hatred of Women and Children, Deliverance from Traumas chapter).

Anna said the spirit guide, under the anti-messiah spirit of Luther, is a controller and a saboteur. I had a divorce, did not graduate from college, and received a Social Security disability in 1990.

Metaxis and other authors document that Martin Luther became anti-Semitic three years before his death, advocating the burning of synagogues and putting the Jewish people into forced labor. Julius Streicher, an antisemitic propagandist who was hung at Nuremberg, loved Luther, published his writings, and turned many Germans against the Jews. [123]

Curses on the Firstborn

> "Through faith, he kept the Passover, and the sprinkling of blood, lest he that destroyed the firstborn should touch them." (Heb. 11:28)
>
> (See also Ex. 12:13 KJV)

Some of the firstborn children in my family have died early or are disabled.

Because the Egyptian trinity, the I H S, has been over our churches and displayed on crosses and altar cloths.

Because we celebrate Easter instead of Passover, and the blood of the Passover lamb is not on the doorposts of our hearts.

Anna said the spirit of Luther brings a curse on the firstborn girl. (See My Story chapter).

Typhon brings a curse on both the firstborn boy and girl. Typhon works with Python, which is over Migraine headaches. Pastor Eloyse believed Typhon to be the voice of Put Satanachia.[124]

Typhon/Merodach is an angel of death that brings the death of communication and trespassing. Typhon is over upper respiratory infections and opposes the deliverance minister.[125] Kitchen says Typhon is a dismembering Freemason god.[126]

If you are a firstborn, cast these curses out of yourself. Cast or proxy these out of your firstborn children.

11

Deliverance from Traumas

A woe is put on those who wrongly use power. (Micah 2:1). It was a Sunday, September 11, 2003, an anniversary of 9-11, when I spoke with a teenager in the back of the RTD bus. She asked for forgiveness for her sins but was still unsure of heaven. Responding to my questions, she said her uncle had been working in a hospital near the World Trade Center, and for three days, the family did not know whether he was dead or alive. After I proxied out shock, trauma, and fear, she knew she would go to heaven when she died. A miracle. This was my first awareness that trauma could block the assurance of eternal life.

In a deliverance session, not as I witness on my morning walks, I cast out traumas, starting at conception, then infancy, as a toddler, preschooler, school age, high school, and present age. Cast out every aspect of the abusive incident and have them forgive the persons involved. In 1999, after I delivered my second husband from many different traumas, Pastor Eloyse noticed his face had changed.

Cast out any of these traumas listed below. Add your own.

- Abuse; emotional, physical, or verbal.
- Infant, child, teen, or adult sexual abuse.
- Rejection or abandonment.
- Not being able to speak up.

- Abuse by a person in authority.
- Domestic Violence.
- Sex trafficked or Satanic Ritually abused.
- Illness, disability, or surgery.
- Trauma in a psych hospital.
- Any abortion.
- An illegally forced abortion.
- Poverty.
- Being homeless or without food.
- Slavery.
- Being hated.
- Racial traumas.
- Being in jail, prison, an ICE prison, or a prison camp.
- Living in a refugee camp.
- Being a refugee.
- Terror in your country.
- War.
- Not having a green card.

Cast out being a Martyr

When Yeshua rules, there will be no persecution.

> "They shall not hurt nor destroy in all my holy mountain." (Is. 11:9)

Jews and those who believe in Yeshua have been Martyrs for many millennia. Especially pastors and missionaries in Catholic, Islamic, Hindu, Buddhist, and Communist countries.

I cast out Martura, an angel of death, as revealed to Pastor Eloyse; It came out with a burp! Cast out the inherited and personal trauma of persecution and becoming a martyr.[127]

Paul asked to know Yeshua, his resurrection's power, and "the fellowship of his suffering." (Philip. 3:10). Cast out for all believers; being hated, severely persecuted, tortured, jailed, killed, beheaded, and even crucified. (Matt. 24:9-10; Rev. 6:9-11).

"Surely he hath borne our griefs, and carried our sorrows."
(Is. 53:4a)

"With his stripes, we are healed."

(Is. 53:5b)

The Defilement of Women in the Confessional and in Private Counseling

God would never forgive Eli's sons, who defiled women in the tabernacle. (1 Sam. 2:12, 22 only KJV). (2 Cor. 6:15 KJV, RVA, RVR1960). Cast out the spirit of Belial; stingy, a homosexual, a rapist, and a murderer. (Judges 19:20-28; 1 Sam. 25:17 KJV, RVR1960). Taylor said Belial "demands sacrifice." (See The 80-list, Appendix E).

We do not need to go through a priest to ask for forgiveness of sins. We can go directly to God, the Father, through Yeshua because the veil in the temple was torn in two when Yeshua died on the cross. (Matt. 27:51).

Chick and Chiniquy say the Catholic confessional is from Babylon and was designed to find out what was going on, to control and blackmail people.[128][129][130]

Chiniquy said priests were commanded to question women in the confessional regarding sexual activities. Chiniquy said only 21 of 200 priests he heard confessions from did not confess to sinning with women. A woman named Mary was so traumatized from sinning with two priests that she had previously "confessed to" that she died young. [131]

Pastors also have abused women whom they were counseling. My kindergarten teacher said she and others left the Lutheran church because the pastor was sinning with women. I can compare the confessional's misuse to the Yokefellow church group counselor and Dr. M.'s sin against me, which brought depression and disability. I kept telling my story. Finally, in 1990, a psychiatrist validated my concerns.

Judith Herman, a psychiatrist who wrote *Trauma and Recovery*, discusses incest victims' trauma, domestic violence, and even survivors of the Holocaust. She advocated without success for the expansion of the diagnosis, Post Traumatic Stress Disorder, PTSD, to include prolonged, repeated trauma, which she calls Complex PTSD. She said idolatry of one's abusers is part of Complex PTSD.[132] (See Lucario, Appendix H).

Beck quotes William Masters, who said these adult-to-adult relationships are like statutory rape due to the imbalance of power. [133]

In Beck's Newsweek article, Gartrell said sexually abused patients "look very much like incest survivors."[134]

Threats of Ex-communication, from the Inquisition to the Molestation of Boys

Bartholomew reports that the Catholic Church had a law of secrecy that dated back to the Inquisitions when persons could secretly inform on a person who was reverting to Jewish biblical traditions. This law also threatened that any priest (or Catholic) who spoke of any secrets, like priests molesting boys, would be excommunicated. This law has recently been negated, but many barriers to justice for the boys remain.[135]

The Lutheran Church Missouri Synod excommunicated me in January 1983 because I had started attending the Assembly of God church. This was the same Lutheran church Dr. M. and his wife attended. This was the same month my teenage children went to live with their father.

Deliverance from the False Doctrines of the Catholic Church

Horn said Pope Boniface VIII was said to have been one of the evilest men who ever lived. He was charged with sodomy after his death. (See Boniface. Appendix.)[136][137]

Years ago, I delivered out of the CLF Boniface pattern before attending a Catholic funeral for a woman whom I had brought to a Messianic congregation. After the deliverances, I felt I could love more.

Yeshua showed me infestations of hatred, and the spirit of Boniface need to be delivered out so the woman from South America to whom I dedicated my book, and all of us, can be free. The hatred comes from mixing the gospel with witchcraft.

(Hatred, see More Curses and Demons to Cast Out, Deliverance from Curses Chapter).

Epigenetics, Traumas in your Genetic Code

There has been intermarriage, especially between the colored races, Hispanics, Africans, and American Indians, so I deal with all of these. (See Have No Other Gods chapter).

Any race or family can have memories of trauma in their genetic code. Inherited traumas can be in one's DNA, from poverty, slavery, the Inquisition, the Holocaust, or war. Cast out Agaliarept and Sargatanas over the trauma. (See The Deliverance List for Familiar Spirits and the 80-list, Appendices G & E).

Pember speaks of the suffering of American Indians, saying their genes and DNA carry memories of trauma, called Epigenetics.138.[138] (See deliverances in App. L & M)

Mandryk says Native Americans are receiving reparations for their suffering. They struggle with hopelessness, poverty, disease, alcoholism, suicide, abuse, and unemployment. [139]

Traumas of Afro-Americans and Recent African Immigrants

Tudor Bismark said the Afro-Americans had inherited the bastard curse from slavery which he believed was the biggest problem for his family and church. Krodeus, over the bastard spirit, is the master curse. He delivered the bastard curse off himself, his boys, and his failing church. Now he has a large church in Africa.[140] (See Valentine's Day and Fornication, Have no Other Gods chapter.)

Many Afro-Americans and recent refugees have been abandoned by or separated from their fathers and experience poverty. Mandryk documents that recent African immigrants may have been in refugee camps where they nearly starved—many suffered terrors from rapes, war, and genocide.[141]

Childhood Traumas

In a teaching on trauma, I learned about "counter will," the instinct to do the exact opposite of what I am told to do. Some do what they are told to do, even if it goes against common sense.

Samuel's and Moses' mothers show us a biblical example of mothers nursing babies, possibly for three to five years. (1 Sam. 1:19-23, Ex. 2:1-10). For at least three generations, babies have not been loved. A neighbor told my grandmother to let my mother cry when she was a newborn. Then her navel ruptured and bled. My mother was taught "strict schedule feeding" at a Lutheran nursing school; to not pick up or touch her crying babies before the four hours was up. This interfered with her instincts to mother and bond with her babies. In nursing school in 1981, we students were to tell the mothers that if they nursed their baby more often than every four hours, they wouldn't have enough milk.

These are cruel teachings. Job speaks of an ostrich that is hardened against her young ones. (Job 39:13-17).

Another woman, ten years older than me, said her mom used strict schedule feeding. She and I both had trouble concentrating on parenting and resisted close relationships. Lucario identifies this as terminal aloneness, second on her list of emotional symptoms of Complex Post-Traumatic Stress Disorder. (See Lucario, Appendix H).

Pediatrician and author Dr. William Sears said these symptoms are typical of those whose mothers practiced Restraint Parenting. He says these children will also be anxious, mistrusting, and angry, and the mother will have difficulty teaching the child spiritual truths. Sears advocates Attachment Parenting, feeding your baby when they cry, wearing and sleeping with your baby. He indicates the father's support is vital for these disciplines and reports that mothers who practice these disciplines have joy in being mothers and usually elect not to return to work. He suggests a part-time job, best in the home, if the mother needs to work.[142] (See References).

The mother who laid on her baby and smothered him in the bible was a prostitute. You are not a prostitute. You can sleep with your baby. (1 Kings 3:16-28).

We must forgive ourselves, nurses, neighbors, mothers, and grandmothers for depriving babies of love.

> *"He shall feed his flock like a shepherd: he shall gather the lambs with his arm, and carry them in his bosom, and shall gently lead those that are with young."* (Is. 40:11 KJV).

Bonding with my daughter was weak because I went to nursing school for a few months when she was a baby. I was more bonded to my son. But when he and his sister moved to their dad's, my daughter took her dresser, but I kept my son's chest of drawers. She told me that it was challenging for him. He often had to clean up his and his step-brothers' room because his clothes were strewn around. I asked Yeshua what spirit caused me to keep my son's chest of drawers. The answer was "Luther. Luther hates boys and children." (See Luther, Deliverance from Curses chapter).

Children may experience other traumas: divorce, child abuse, child sexual abuse, neglect, abandonment, isolation, starvation, strict schedule feeding, female genital mutilation, pornography, homelessness, sex trafficking, war, death of a parent or sibling, and school shootings. These can bring mental illness, physical illness, anorexia, use of illegal drugs, alcoholism, sexual identity confusion, and early death.

Don't let the media be a babysitter. The child is desensitized to sin by seeing homosexuality, sex, violence, and witchcraft on computers, TV, or their phones. Even Christian programs for children can have hidden witchcraft. Irene Park says puppets, used in many programs, are witchcraft. (Puppets, see Concern about Curses, Know You Have Eternal Life chapter).

Hatred of Women and Children

CLF knew that Put Satanachia and Nebiros are principalities over both homosexuality and hatred of women. One cannot separate women from their children. So, these are also over hatred of children. I believe they are also in opposition to the gospel. (See Miracle Homosexual Deliverance, Appendix F).

Yeshua, knew women and children would be abused. He said,

> *"Daughters of Jerusalem, weep not for me, but weep for yourselves, and for your children."* (Luke 23:28)

Pastor Eloyse, examined Susan Forward's book, *Men Who Hate Women and the Women Who Love Them*, and said these behaviors against women are under the principality of Nebiros.[143]

Forward, speaking of couples she counseled, said misogynist men, in a long-term relationship, do everything they can to destroy the woman they profess to love deeply.[144]

Results of Child Sexual Abuse

I received disability in 1990 for depression and PTSD, and I see a psychiatrist yearly. I have trouble receiving gifts. It upsets me when my husband brings so many groceries home that I can barely get all the frozen food in the freezer. I pick on and file my fingernails and cuticles. Because I clench my teeth at night, I wear an inexpensive bite guard. I am allergic to dairy and gluten and have degenerative disc disease in my spine but little pain. My arthritis doctor said I am in the one percent of people who have been healed of fibromyalgia. I thank deliverance. Close relationships are difficult for me. I know only a few names of people at church. I tend to want to care for people and ignore my needs. Fasting can be difficult because of the strict schedule feeding when I was a baby. A nurse explained it was because I was already stressed. I can fast drinking broth. Dave Bryan recommends fasting 3 days a month.

Survivors of trauma need regular sleep, nutrition, reduction of stress, and attention to being safe. Many have physical illnesses, diabetes, pain, insomnia, and some are overweight. Many are estranged from their families. Many persons on disability for mental illness have one or more secret order bondages; infant baptism, freemasonry, Scouting, or military. They live in nursing homes, assisted living homes, with families, or in their apartments.

Results of Child Sexual Abuse of Boys

Stewart said he and his family were in denial about his and his brother's sexual abuse by his Boy Scout leader. He couldn't deal with it until he was forty years old and still had nightmares.[145]

Hegstrom tells of his failure in his attempt to tell his mother about the sexual abuse by a teacher. As Judith Herman reports, his story exposes the violence that can occur in intimate relationships after being abused as a child. He overcame abusive anger against his wife and women, remarried his wife, reparented his children, and founded an organization that rehabilitated abusive men. A daughter is heading Life Skills International.[146][147]

Schizophrenia, PTSD and CPTSD

Rich Buhler had received 40,000 phone calls and had 5,000 guests on his nationwide radio talk show. He realized that behind lethargy, depression, and anger, are physical and emotional victimization, and sexual abuse. This victimization may have been documented but ignored by counselors.[148]

Buhler writes that Dr. Mohan Nair, a child psychiatrist, believed that most adult mental health problems, even the diagnosis of schizophrenia, are the result of child abuse.[149][150]

Mark Hemans and other deliverance ministers have delivered people from demons of Schizophrenia. (See Put Satanachia, the 80-list, Appendix E. Hemans, See References).

Post-traumatic stress disorder (PTSD), as described in the ICD 11, may develop following exposure to an extremely threatening or horrific event or series of events.[151]

Complex post-traumatic stress disorder (Complex PTSD) in the ICD 11, is described as a disorder that may develop following exposure to an event or series of events of an extremely threatening or horrific nature, most commonly prolonged or repetitive events from which escape is difficult or impossible.[152] (CPTSD, See Lucario, Appendix H).

12

How I Speak with People Who Need the Savior

On my morning walks, a Seventh Day Adventist woman I met three times said she can't always get people to repent of their sins, so she asks them to say "yes" to Jesus.

A Catholic woman from Eritrea I met at the laundromat said "yes" to "Yesu" and his blood to wash her sins away.

A Catholic woman who wasn't sure of going to heaven said yes to the blood of Jesus to wash her sins away.

I speak to one person at a time. I write down the first name of the person I am speaking to on a piece of paper I carry in my fanny pack. When asking them questions, I will jot down their answers and transfer the answer to a prayer letter that I send to several persons.

No matter their answers, I usually move to the next question.

To know if I was speaking to a Jewish person, I used to ask if I could tell them the name of the Savior in Hebrew.

- I want you to be sure you will go to heaven when you die. May I talk to you about that? Some people will say, "not today," or "I'm good," because they do not want to speak with me. Others have told me they do not believe in Jesus and practice certain types of witchcraft.

- If they say "yes," I ask, what did the Savior do 2000 years ago so you can go to heaven? Many people know that Yeshua died for our sins on the cross, but many of these people are not sure of going to heaven!
- Do you believe that there is a heaven and a hell?
- Where do you believe your soul and spirit will go when you die?
- If they say "to heaven," I will ask why they believe they will go to heaven.
- If they say something about believing in Yeshua, Jesus (their name for the Savior), I know they are saved and sure of heaven. Another good answer was from a Catholic man from near Juarez who said he was going to heaven because he had repented of his sins!

A few people going to good churches have said they are going to hell. Some of these people will not accept the Savior or deliverance. These people need to be delivered from curses that brought condemnation as comes with abortions. (See Appendix D). The only unforgivable sin is blasphemy against the Holy Spirit. (Mark 3:28-29).

If they or their parents have had the infant or sprinkling baptism (or the Mormon immersion), they usually say they hope to go to heaven, or "it depends." This is an example of the Catholic Church wrongfully teaching that one can never be sure of eternal life and the blockage of assurance of eternal life by curses from the infant or sprinkling baptism.

A doctor said he hoped he would not go to purgatory.

They may say they are going to heaven because they are good. I usually tell them that Yeshua wants us to be good.

He said, "If you love me, keep my commandments." (John 14:15 NKJV).

Some may say they are going to heaven because they believe in God. However, better said, because they believe in God the Son, Yeshua, Jesus, who died for their sins.

A man from the mid-east only said God told him he would go to heaven.

I will ask them to accept the Savior

I will ask if they want to say "yes" to the Savior and his blood to wash away their sins.

If they say, "yes," I ask them what name they want to use for the Savior, explaining that the name Yeshua translates as "Savior."

Do they want to use the short prayer or the longer Ten Commandments prayer?

It is best to use the more extended Ten Commandments prayer when asking people to repent of their sins because the first commandments prohibit having, making, bowing down to, and serving other gods. (Ex. 20:1-60). After reading the first two commandments, I will ask, "What gods have you worshiped? What religions have you and your family been into?"

I ask if they want to say "no" to that bondage and ask for forgiveness. If they won't, it may be counterproductive to continue.

The bondages some people have not been able to renounce, aside from infant baptism and praying to Mary, are rock music, the 33rd degree Masonry, a lifetime Order of the Arrow organization, Yoga, attending the Mosque, Hare Krishna, and Hindu gods. For example, a woman could not part with the Buddha her grandmother gifted her.

You may print out my Ten Commandments prayer or the Ten Commandments from an online Bible. Carrying these in a cellophane sleeve will preserve the page. It is easier to carry the gospel tract "The Best Story," which summarizes the Ten Commandments.[153]

The Ten Commandments Prayer
Exodus 20:1-17

Forgive me for my sins. I forgive those who have sinned against me. (Matt. 6:12).

1. Forgive me for rejecting you as the Father, Son, and Holy Spirit.

2. Forgive me for having, making, bowing down to, and serving graven images and anything you have created in the heavens, on the earth, or under the sea. Forgive me for making idols in my heart. (Ez. 14:1-11).

3. Forgive me for taking your name in vain (Blasphemy or cussing). (Use the name Yeshua.)

4. Forgive me for not remembering your Sabbath day and keeping it holy.

5. Forgive me for not honoring my mother, father, and authorities. (1 Tim. 2:2). (I have them forgive their parents if they were abandoned, neglected, or abused by them.)

6. *"Thou shalt not kill."* (Ex. 20:13 KJV; Matt 5:21-22, 1 John 3:15). Forgive me for hate, holding on to my anger, calling names, and murder. Forgive me for using birth control that may have killed babies, or abortion.

7. *"Thou shalt not commit adultery."* Forgive me for adultery, fornication, lust, sex sins, & for looking at pornography & nudity. (Ex. 20:14 KJV; Matt. 5:27-28; Gal. 5:19).

8. Forgive me for stealing and for not giving a tithe, ten percent to God. (Mal. 3:8-10).

9. Forgive me for being a false witness or lying about my neighbor.
10. Forgive me for coveting or wanting what belongs to other people.

Ask them to repent of any other sins silently. Pastor Eloyse said cast out the spirit of sin and ask people to pause and receive their forgiveness.

- I receive the blood of Yeshua to wash my sins and cleanse me. (Ps. 51:2; 1 Peter 1:17-19).
- Holy Spirit, come into my spirit. *"For Yochanan (John) used to immerse people in water; but in a few days, you will be immersed in the Ruach HaKodesh, (the Holy Spirit)!"* (Acts 1:5 CJB) (See also John 6:63).
- Give me the courage to live and witness for you. *"Fear none of those things which thou shalt suffer: ... be thou faithful unto death, and I will give thee a crown of life."* (Rev. 2:10).

The Shorter Matthew 22:36-39 Prayer

In the Name of Yeshua, forgive my sins against the Father, The Son, and the Holy Spirit. Forgive me for my sins against my neighbor, myself, and my family. (Also see Lev. 19:17-18).

Salvation and Deliverance are Needed if People Are Not Sure About Going to Heaven

If they say they hope to go to heaven or are unsure about it, I ask about some bondages. Did they or their parents have the infant baptism or go to Semana Santa or other ceremonies? Was anyone in the family in Scouting or Freemasonry, or have they been sleeping with their girl/woman or boy/male friend? Are they unforgiving, or have they been traumatized?

13

Deliverances as I Witness

A person is more apt to understand the need to renounce infant baptism if I read the verses about being redeemed by the blood of the Messiah. One must believe before being immersed. Biblical baptism is immersion. (Mark 16:16a, Matt. 3:16).

I ask, do you want to say "yes" to the blood of Yeshua and "no" to the curse that came from infant baptism? (I may name, Luciferina, Isis, and Krodeus).

When witnessing, I verbalize the prayer first, asking them to listen. Then I ask them to repeat the deliverance prayer, phrase by phrase, with me.

I will tell the person to say, "Go, in the name of Yeshua." I explained that if they ate some spoiled food, they might vomit. Because deliverance is spiritual, they may get yawn, cough, or burp as the spirit comes out. I will say, "go, get out of (their first name) in the name of Yeshua."

Do they want to say "no" to being a sacrifice because of the cross drawn on their brow and breast?

Do they want to say "no" to praying to Mary, really Isis? Some people will renounce their infant baptism but will not renounce praying to Mary.

I usually tell them they have become a citizen of the Vatican at confirmation.[154] Do they want to cast this out and choose to be a heaven citizen? (Daniel 12:1; Luke 10:20).

Fornication

Fornication is having sexual relations before marriage, which is a major reason, aside from infant baptism, why people are not sure about going to heaven.

"For this, you know that no fornicator, unclean person, nor covetous man, who is an idolater, has any inheritance in the kingdom of Christ and God." (Eph. 5:5).

One man prayed and was still unsure of heaven. He was going to a good church but sleeping with his fiancée. I said this is fornication; they should repent, separate for a time, get marriage counseling, and get married. (Eph. 5:3).

Abandonment by Father

David said, *"thou art a helper of the fatherless"*. (Ps. 10:14)

I usually ask if someone's father was there for them. If not, cast out the trauma of abandonment by the father. Sometimes the mothers are absent. Cast out the curse of Molech. This curse is the last word in the Old Testament. (Mal. 4:5-6). (Mal'akhi 3:23-24 CJB).

Children are like strawberries. If you ignore them, they will turn rotten.

Unforgiveness

Yeshua told me my sins will not be forgiven if I do not forgive. (Matt. 6:12, 14-15).

Anna believed the first thing to deliver in a counseling session is unforgiveness because it brings diseases. Ask, "Who has hurt you?" She said it is difficult for them to acknowledge whom they have hurt. [155]

I asked a woman on the train if she was mad at anyone. She said a lot of people had hurt her. I cast out the trauma of abuse. Cast out the demon spirits, Baal, Reoseles and Fleurety, over unforgiveness. I use The Deliverance List for Familiar Spirits if I have trouble forgiving a person. (See Appendix G).

Do not believe that forgiveness is all a person needs to be healed from traumas. People need deliverance! Yeshua healed and delivered women who followed him, including Mary Magdelene. (Luke 8:1-3).

Trauma

Many homeless persons or persons with disability acknowledge they were abused or molested as a child. Cast out this trauma. It is good if you have time with them to minister this deliverance. If the person is Afro-American, I cast out the inherited trauma of slavery.

Practicing Various Sins

Abortion

Women tell me in private about these traumas, but I asked an unbalanced woman who had gone across the street, escaping from a house of prostitution, if she had an abortion, as we went through the Ten Commandments prayer. Her pimp arrived and was angry at me. (See Deliverance from Abortion, Birth Control. Appendix D).

Curses Bring Addiction to Drugs, Alcohol, Sex Sins, and the Media

I usually ask people if they practice any of these now or if they did in the past. If they are or did in the past, they need repentance, salvation, and deliverance. If they do that in the present, they also need to stop these practices. Drugs and alcohol. Sexual sins, pornography on cell phones or other media, computer games, bad TV and movies, or rock music. Playing cards.

Deliver out curses of Luciferina and Krodeus, the secret orders and traumas behind these addictions. Cast out the spirits you took in from the sin; the idolatry of the person or the substance, the familiar spirits, what your idol said or sang, the name of the drug or alcoholic beverage, and what you experienced or did while using it. Deliver out The Deliverance List for Familiar Spirits, Appendix G.

One person believes he is going to hell; another is not sure of going to heaven. Both blamed their sins when they were alcoholics 20-30 years ago. (Gal. 5:21; Eph. 5:18).

The use of wine and strong drinks by priests in the temple is forbidden. We are New Testament kings and priests. (Lev. 10:9; Rev. 1:6a). We are to be filled with the Holy Spirit, not drunk with alcohol. (Eph. 5:18a). Grape juice should be used for "the cup" with the bread, not wine. Keep alcohol out of your home. I saw a boy with some of the wine used for the "cup" on the Sabbath. He took it to his room and drank it.

The person who wants deliverance will need to trust experienced counselors, maybe rehab centers. Yeshua does bring miracle deliverance, though. Addictions to various substances, even medications prescribed by a doctor, could make a person take the beast's mark and go to hell. But do not stop taking your medications or encourage a person in medical or psychiatric treatment to stop taking their medications unless they receive confirmation of healing. If they have a serious mental illness, they could then require hospitalization. Cast out side effects of these meds, which is how "Satan comes to collect." (The beast's mark, See Prologue).

The more deliverance you receive, the less you will be dependent on drugs, alcohol, and medications. Aim to get free now so you will go up in the Rapture.

14

How to Keep a Person from Falling Away

from Salvation and Deliverance

The person involved must fellowship with believers, continue receiving deliverance, and read the Bible daily to stay free. (Luke 11:14-26). David Bryan, advocates both deliverance and discipleship. (See Instructions Regarding the Deliverances. See References).

I ministered deliverance to one woman in 2004, but she did not continue receiving more deliverance that Pastor Eloyse knew she needed. Eleven to fifteen years later, three times, the demons came back to attack her, and finally me. In June 2022, Yeshua told me to cancel the lies that have been said about me. Immediately, she repented for what she had said. She also renounced a false religion and returned to Bible study, accepting deliverances.

Many people go to church but don't read the Bible. This set of people needs deliverance from inherited hatred of God. In the morning of January 1, 2011, I began reading the New Testament portion in a one-year Bible with my husband. (Eph. 5:25-27). I added two other persons. One came to my home, and the other was on the phone. I led them in putting on their armor from Ephesians 6 and ministered deliverance from fears and imaginations. Another woman is reading with these two and added two others. I added a family member, another woman, and several others who don't read daily. (2 Cor. 1:1-5).

As I read the Bible, I replace Jesus with Yeshua and Christ with Messiah or HaMashiach. The King James Version is superior in many ways, because even the New King James Version has footnotes to question important verses like Mark 16:9-20. I do use the New King James Version. Many other new Bible versions leave out important words, even verses. The NIV omits, "He has sent me to heal the broken hearted" in Luke 4:18.

Bring them to church and Bible study and pray for them to receive the Holy Spirit with the evidence of speaking in tongues. (Acts 2:4, 10:44-46, 19:6). If they find it challenging to speak in tongues, deliverance from the counterfeit Holy Spirit and other demons is needed. (See The 80-list).

Conclusion

Will you Recognize the Messiah? Isaiah Describes Him

"The people that walked in darkness have seen a great light: they that dwell in the land of the shadow of death, upon them hath the light shined. For unto us a child is born, unto us a son is given: and the government shall be upon his shoulder: and his name shall be called Wonderful, Counsellor, The mighty God, The everlasting Father, The Prince of Peace. Of the increase of his government and peace there shall be no end, upon the throne of David, and upon his kingdom, to order it, and to establish it with judgment and with justice from henceforth even for ever. The zeal of the Lord of hosts will perform this." (Is. 9:2, 6-7, Yesha'Yahu 9:1, 5-6). (Also Is. 11:1-5).

Be Proactive

Be courageous when you are looking for a new medical or psychiatric provider. Ask their sexual preference. Ask the teachers of your children. Some of these teachers are witches! Of course, ask them to accept the Savior.

In the church you attend, train several persons or group leaders to personally question each adult attendee to see if they are sure of going to heaven, and minister to them if they are not. Some of them may secretly be witches! (See Questionnaire, chapter five).

Before deciding to stay at a new church, or in the church you attend, I suggest doing a lot of spiritual warfare around the property. Ask the persons in leadership if they are sure of going to heaven using my questions. Ascertain that they believe in the Holy Spirit, deliverance, spiritual warfare, and speaking in tongues. (2 Tim. 3:5). Discern if women are honored and given permission to speak up and teach. More information may be gained by attending mid-week meetings. Ask who owns the building. Persons of wealth may be Freemasons.

Traditions

The serpent in the garden asks, "hath God said." (Gen. 3:1). The serpent, Python, deceived us. We have eaten the forbidden fruit. We have not even regarded the Ten Commandments. We have changed God's law to fit the traditions of our families, churches, and countries. As Park said, "we defend the sin." Many of our "Fixed Delusions" have come from inherited curses. These may cause us to miss the rapture or worse, be deceived, take the Mark of the Beast, and go to Hell!

From the cross, Yeshua said, *"Father, forgive them for they know not what they do."* (Luke 23:34a).

The pastor in Arvada brought a guest speaker who said no one witnessed to him until he was in prison. Who will go? Who will minister to the masses, the mentally ill, the developmentally disabled, and the homeless? (Luke 14:12-14).

I love Yeshua. I asked him about my incomplete deliverance at CLF. The answer:

> *"But we have this treasure in earthen vessels, that the excellency of the power may be of God, and not of us."*
>
> (2 Cor. 4:7)

Be Strong and Do Exploits

In 1996 my husband and I moved to a condo in Denver. This area would be my internship for witnessing for Yeshua and spiritual warfare. In 2015 and 2017, Pastor Eloyse's daughter gave me deliverance files to use for deliverance. These became valuable for my own deliverance, proxy deliverances, and spiritual warfare.

Deliverance from traumas and secret orders I suffered under have brought this book to you. I hope to publish a subsequent book in Spanish and then publish the entirety of My Story.

> Apostle Paul told Timothy, *"For God hath not given us the spirit of fear, but of power, and of love, and of a sound mind. Be not thou therefore ashamed of the testimony of our Lord, nor of me his prisoner: but be thou partaker of the afflictions of the gospel according to the power of God; Who hath saved us, and called us with a holy calling, not according to our works, but according to his own purpose and grace, which was given us in Christ Jesus before the world began."* (2 Tim. 1:7-9)

Satan accuses us day and night.

> *"And they overcame him by the blood of the Lamb, and by the word of their testimony, and they loved not their lives unto the death."* (Rev. 12:10b,11)

> *"The people that do know their God shall be strong, and do exploits."* (Dan. 11:32b)

Appendices

A. Deliverance from Infant Baptism and the Order of the Arrow.

Anna Paraseah. March 14, 2006.

Repent of your sins and deliver this out.

Anna recorded that many demons enter with the curse of Luciferina at infant baptism. There is a blockage to knowing God.[156]

The result of Infant baptism is victimization.

The person is lured into another form of witchcraft, like the Boy Scout Order of the Arrow.

The Cub, Boy and Girl Scouts bring hatred (even of God) and lust. (Ex. 20:5).

(The sun god Osiris and Baphomet enter with witchcraft orders like the Order of the Arrow bringing more victimization).

There is rape. Demonic avoidance of intimacy follows.

The abuse causes the youth to be fearful of people.

Any trauma brings unforgiveness. Unforgiveness brings illnesses.[157] The principality of Fleurety is over rejecting love. (See The 80-list, Appendix E).

(Beelzebub, the false father, over uncleanness), causes the person to be demoralized and have no happiness.

Negativity results under the (sun) god Baal.

The god, Merodach/Typhon, brings the death of communication and trespassing.

Apollyon and Abaddon, two Angels of Death, enter. (Rev. 9:11).

Cast out the trinity under Satan; Beelzebub, Astaroth, and Put Satanachia. (John 10:10).

Cast out the Eastern Star spirits. (Women's Freemasonry, Girl Scout, or Girl Guide spirits). (See Appendix J).

It all goes back to idolatry. A person must have something to worship. Lucifer brings the demand for perfection in self. (Isaiah 14:13-14). Cast out idolatry and the image of self as perfect.

Cast out the demand for perfection that came when the youth was Confirmed in the church, and as a compensation for the shame of sexual abuse.

Adding to Anna's deliverance, there are four spirits to cast out if you or a family member was inducted into this order, from the Boy Scouts of America, Order of the Arrow Handbook, 1991,

1. The Mighty Chief (of the fire), Allowat Sakima. Service. "The day of (hard) work."

2. The Medicine Man, Meteu. Brotherhood. "He reminds us to love one another." Silence.

3. The Guard of the Circle, Nitiket. Cheerfulness. Scant food test.

4. The Guide, Kichkinet. Helpfulness and Friendliness. "Spend the night alone."

(The Medicine Man, see, Can a Christian Have a Demon? Teaching on Actual Deliverance chapter).

B. Boniface Deliverance Pattern.[158]

You may benefit from this deliverance, as I did, even if you have never been Catholic.

Repent of your sins and deliver this out.

Deliverance from the False Doctrines of the Catholic Church titled "Boniface."

Boniface is a spirit over false doctrine and error in the Catholic Church.

Luther is over false doctrine in the Protestant church.

Boniface is a spirit under Lucifer & Ashteroth.

Boniface = brilliant face.

"Many (demons) works under me."

A false doctrine of the church overrides the family's authority of mothers and fathers over their children.

The False Doctrine of Mary, the Mother of God

"God the Father wed Mary through immaculate conception,"

She became the mother of God.

The assumption as Queen of heaven.

She became the authority over the father.

The Rosary

Preaching Mary

Prayers to Mary

Feasts of Mary

False prayer spirit. The guiding spirit is Demetrius.

False belonging

False security

False adoration

Appendices

Idolatry of:
- Pearls
- Statutes
- Holy cards
- Incense
- Candles
- Outdoor shrines (church houses).
- Priestly rings
- Robes
- Virgin robes (men's)
- Saints
- Medallions
- A blessing (dedication) card
- Holy waters
- Blessing with holy water

False Doctrine of Infant Baptism

False Doctrine of Purity, A Doctrine of Legalism.

The whole religion Emphasizes Purity. Catholics must be pure.

Mary is pure and has no children. (See Matt. 1:24-25).

Joseph is pure because he never touched Mary sexually.

Joseph is a saint.

Sainthood is due to purity.

"He is so holy."

Eating fish on Friday to be pure.

False purity.

Every Catholic practice centers around this doctrine, even the Bible.

We have our own Bible because all other Bibles are wrong.

We have "imprimatur" - this book is without error.

We have "nihilobstat." nothing is wrong. Nihilobstat.

The doctrine of Mary only

Mary is purer than the Father because "there is no Father."

Catholics must be pure like Mary.

The belief in the Trinity is a token, a cover-up.

There is no other church.

Peter is the rock upon which the church is built. (See John 1:42).

The belief that Apostle Peter left his wife. (See Matt. 8:14).

In Mark 10:29, 30. All versions but KJV omits "has left wife."

Catholic priests usually have no wives.

This is a program to cause believers to seek to obtain a position as high as Mary, higher than the Father, to use the body of Christ to usurp the Father's authority.

The False Doctrine of the Assumption of Mary.

Mary was pure. She ascended to heaven.

The False Doctrine of the Apostles

There are only 12 apostles. There can't be anymore. (See 1 Cor. 15: 5-9 KJV).

False Doctrine of Martyrdom.

Mary sacrificed her life. She had no children.

A false sacrifice of life.

Martyrdom is the highest good. God expects us to sacrifice our life in death.

Become a saint by being a martyr.

The highest goal of a Catholic is to become a martyr. (See Rom. 12:1; 1 Peter 1:18-19).

Priests and Kings

There are only a few priests. There are only a few kings.

Each parish has a priest. You must belong to a parish to receive doctrine.

There is no doctrine anywhere except "we have everything orders."

Vestments

The robes, cloaks, are to conceal, hide the truth, to cloak the eyes, ears, mind, & brain. (See 2 Kings 10:22).

Hatred of Women

Men have superiority over women

Women can't teach because "we hate women."

They create impossible situations.

The Good Qualities of Women

Women are strong, meek, and have strength & character.

They are too loyal and faithful. They won't compromise.

The Ritual Mass

A false sacrifice.

Through the ritual, the mass causes believers to worship the creation more than the creator. This Brings a reprobate mind. (Rom. 1:25, 28).

The Wine & Wafer. Adoration of the body of Jesus, not Jesus.

Transubstantiation.

The Spirit of the Pope

Universalism. The false doctrine of the Universal Church.

The Roman church shall rule over the whole church, for everyone shall accept the "true" Church and give allegiance to the church in Rome.

This doctrine comes out of the Roman church. It is the theological doctrine that all souls will eventually find salvation in the grace of God. All Roman Catholics shall be in heaven.

Humanism

The study of humanities stemmed from studying classical Greek and Latin literature and culture during the Middle Ages. It was one of the factors given to the rise of the Renaissance. Emphasis on human interests. A focus on self-life. Religion is a cover-up for self-life.

C. More Deliverances for the Sephardic Jews, other Jews and Believers

As I write this, I get, "I'm not in here. I'm not going to leave."

Persecution began soon after Yeshua returned to heaven, starting with Stephen. (Acts 7:54-60). Inherited trauma in your DNA, Epigenetics, may extend from the Inquisitions in Europe, in the New World, in a communist or Islamic country, to the present persecution that accelerated during the lockdowns of COVID-19. (See Cast out being a Martyr, Deliverance from Traumas chapter). Cast out the names of the Popes.

Discard all six-pointed stars and cast out these two trinities. (See the Six-Pointed Star, Symbols and Emblems that Bring Curses chapter).

Cast out Bastit, a spirit over Jewish unbelief. A CLF pattern said a demon spirit, Bastit, came from Egypt and from not evicting all the Canaanites from the promised land. Cast out spiritual blindness that rejects the gospel. (Rom. 11:8, 10, 25).

Cast out:

A Santos religion and worship of saints.

Santeria. (See the Chick booklet, "Evil Eyes.") [159]

Santa Muerte. (The goddess of death).

Santo Niño de Cebú- A Feast Day for The Christ Child.

Watch John Ramirez's YouTube, exposing Witchcraft and Catholic beliefs.[160]

Anna said Greek and Roman gods and goddesses could also be delivered out.

D. Deliverance from Abortion, Birth Control, and other Unbiblical Practices

One hundred years ago, women would smother their unwanted newborn, put the baby in a shoebox, and drop it in the outhouse! An older woman with fifteen siblings said she heard a neighbor criticize her mother for having many children. Her mother said she wasn't like some women she saw carrying a shoe box to the outhouse.

When Park taught at a summer camp, she discerned that I had three babies in heaven. I used the birth control pill and the IUD when I was dating and married to my first husband.[161][162]

Vasectomies and tubal ligations don't kill babies, but God hates them. (Gen. 1:28). Cast out death spirits in the womb after using birth control or abortion. Cast out the witchcraft curse of abortion and the use of birth control in past generations. Stop it from passing to children and grandchildren. Cast out the Druid trinity. (See The Worship of Freemason gods).

Mentally ill and homeless women and others have been traumatized by abortions, miscarriages, and the loss of children. These women may struggle with terrors, insomnia, physical pain, and overeating. In private or trusted group deliverance sessions, cast out the trauma and sins of abortion and birth control methods.

In acknowledgments I said Mark Heman's ministry closely resembles the ministry of Yeshua. The Holy Spirit showed the group prayer helper at the end of Heman's Online meeting on March 18, 2022, the loss of my grandchild "was an injustice." My future daughter-in-law had surgery to remove her large intestine in September 1997. The next day their baby was stillborn. March 18 was ten years and a day after my granddaughter had died in a car accident. Yeshua, came to heal our broken hearts. (Luke 4:18).

Deliverance and Healing for a Woman who had an Abortion.[163]

Deliver these all out with compassion.

The woman who this was intended for got these deliverances 18 years later.

To get the memories, lay hands on the woman's mind. Lose the memories.

Relive the emotional experience.

(Cast out all the negative things you remember).

Cast out the guilt, shame, and embarrassment.

Cast out the trauma of the abortion and what she went through; she will never forget (but can be healed of the trauma).

Cast out:

1. Constant guilt.

2. Condemnation.

3. Damnation is the last stage of condemnation; She may have a fear of going to hell.

Get the father's name. Cast out the spirit of the father of the baby. Use The Deliverance List for Familiar Spirits. (Appendix G).

(Cast out the trauma of rape, if it was a rape).

(Cast out the demons that came in, including the death angel, Molech. See Appendix K).

Say to the mother that when she is delivered, she will be relieved that:

1. The baby went to heaven.

2. Angels trained the baby.

3. She will be united with her child again.

Naming the baby is a positive way to heal.

Other Unbiblical Practices

Don't sign a "Living Will" or a "Five Wishes" document. Better is the National Right to Life "Will to Live," an advanced directive that lists persons who will make your medical decisions if you cannot. (See References to download a "Will to Live").

Hospices use morphine which induces a coma and an earlier death.

Cremation is a Hindu practice and is also wrong because our bones will rise in the rapture when the trumpet blows. Sealed caskets do not allow the body to dry out. (See The Fall Feasts, The Biblical Feasts and Sabbaths are for Today chapter. Hindu, see The Worship of Freemason gods, Have No Other Gods chapter).

E. The 80-List, Eight Principalities

Terry Taylor, a Satanic Priest, submitted this list of eighty demons to the Tattler for the Spring 1974 special edition on Exorcism. He believed Satan was real and these spirits could take over the human body. This is a good list for deliverance and spiritual warfare.

Taylor lists nine superior spirits, descriptions of their positions and works, and 72 major infernal demons with brief descriptions of their works.[164] Taylors text is in quotes. I have added more including from CLF and the Bible.

Pastor Eloyse discerned that #2 to #9 are the principalities in Ephesians 6:12. In 2008, realizing I was not fully delivered, she instructed me to get the eight superior spirits out. She said these are over a "hard heart." (Zech. 7:12; Mark 16:14). (2 Cor 4:7).

Six demons on the 80-list are in the Bible. Satan, Beelzebub, Astaroth, Baal (Jer. 19:5), Balam (Balaam. Rev. 2:14 KJV), and Belial.

#1. "Satan, who serves as emperor of the Grand Grimoire." (Luke 10:18; John 10:10).

#2 "Beelzebub, (or Beelzebuth), his prince."

The ruler of the demons. (Matt. 12:24 NKJV). The strong man. (Luke 11:21). An unclean spirit. (Luke 11:24, also see Luke 11:15-19; 2 Kings 1:2.). Beelzebub is a "false father" over insanity, diseases, viruses, bacteria, and stench. One way that Beelzebub comes in is with molestation. [165]

#3. "Astaroth, the Grand Duke." (Ashtoreth, Ashtaroth). (1 Kings 11:5 NIV).

#4. "Put Satanachia serves as commander-in-chief under Satan and has the power of subjecting all wives and mothers to his wishes, of doing with them as he wills. He provides familiars for mortals and has all knowledge of the planets, past, and future."

"Subjecting wives and mothers" cause children to not be able to love their mothers, and they may even abuse them. In addition, when a man marries and his wife becomes a mother, he may abuse or abandon her and the children.

This author believes another name for Put Satanachia is Baphomet. Two occultist authors call Baphomet the body of the Holy Ghost[166] or the body of the Holy Spirit.[167] Baphomet, half goat and the other half trans-sexual, both male, and female, is popular among homosexuals and in witchcraft.

Kitchen says Baphomet is a freemason god over "Seduction, Lust, Uncleanness." She identifies curses of cancer over 18 parts of the body because of freemasonry oaths.168 Child abuse, sex sins, Krodeus, Python, Beelzebub, Put Satanachia, Agaliarept, and opposing the gospel bring cancer. Tumors came from mixing religions, putting the Ark of God into the temple of Dagon. (1 Sam. 5:1-12).

The third name for Put Satanachia is Shiva, of the Hindu trinity. [169]

Anna documents, Put Satanachia is the false Holy Spirit. He brings false doctrines and familiar or guide spirits, is over computers, hate of God, self-hate, torment, torture, suicide, insanity, paranoid schizophrenia, anorexia, self-destruction, and more. Some ways he enters are by true guilt through past sex life and inherited guilt. Anna said most families have Put Satanachia.[170]

Put Satanachia sits on a person's will, which is part of the soul, so we can't do what we want to do. (Gal. 5:17). One man would not say yes to the Savior until I taught him about using his will. You use your will to get up in the morning. Use your will and choose to say yes to Yeshua.

#5, Agaliarept, Satan's Commander, controls Europe and Asia Minor. He has the power to control past and future and creates animosity between men to create enemies."

Agaliarept is a liar and comes in from fear, inherited or personal occult worship, and sexual trauma or sin.[171]

#6, "Fleurety, Beelzebuth's lieutenant general, controls Africa and performs evil dealings on men at night. Controls a large army of evil familiars, knows about poisonous and hallucinating herbs, controls and causes world wars, and puts lust in man's mind."

#7. "Sargatanas, Astaroth's Brigadier Major, causes mortals to lose memory and transports them to other parts of the world. He watches the going on in private homes, enters into all persons' secret thoughts, and controls many large armies of spirits."

Sargatanas, Lethe and Alexis, Isis, Osiris, and three other spirits are over depression.[172] Zireck is over Bipolar depression and hostility, which enters because of a broken heart.[173]

A child said Zurg (Zireck) came in from the "Toy Story 2" movie. Cast these spirits out from young people who play video games like "Game Boy" and the Xbox, shooting real-looking soldiers. Pray they will be delivered from inherited curses, rejection, and unforgiveness for their parents.

#8. "Nebiros, Astaroth's field marshal, controls North America, can inflict evil on whoever he wishes, controls the power passed by the Hand of Glory, and turn all animals vicious for his means," Anna said the Hand of Glory is the hand of a murderer.

Nebiros brings head knowledge, like a catechism, and freemasonry, especially the Shrine. There is a noose around the neck. It is over nihilism, rebellion, and anarchy.[174] (See Hatred of Women and Children, Deliverance from Traumas chapter, and Appendices F & J).

#9 Lucifuge Roficale, the prime minister, has charge of all wealth and riches, inflicts invisibility, causes earthquakes, destroys religious deities, inflicts diseases and physical defects."

This principality comes in with abuse, brings poverty, attacks those who minister the gospel, and, like Zombies, brings fear of giving and receiving love.[175]

72 major infernal demons (in order of importance):

Baal imparts invisibility.

Agares causes earthquakes.

Vassago, the seer, declares things past, present and future.

Gamygyn controls souls in sin.

Marbas causes diseases.

Valefor influences theft.

Amon and Barbatos, both seers.

Paimon, subjects men to his will.

Buer controls poisons and drugs.

Gusion, a seer.

Sytry produces nudity.

Beleth, a vicious entity, controls lust.

Lerajie causes war.

Eligor causes war and lust.

Zepar drives women mad.

Botis, a seer.

Bathin controls poisons and the disappearance of men and cities.

Saleos controls lust.

Purson, a seer.

Morax governs poisons and herbal drugs.

Ipos creates false courage.

Aini is responsible for destruction by fire.

Naberius, teacher of the sciences and astrology.

Appendices

Glasyalabolas, influences all homicides and incites bloodshed.

Bune changes burial places of the dead.

Bonobe speaks in different tongues.

Berith, a seer.

Astaroth councils and directs fallen angels.

Forneus twists the truth by the usage of different tongues.

Foras controls poisons, herbal drugs and inflicts invisibility on man.

Asmoday guards the hidden treasures.

Gaap transports men from place to place.

Furfur controls thunder, lightning and strong winds.

Marcosias, a strong demon and faithful helper to the exorcist who can conjure.

Solas (or Stolas) controls knowledge of astronomy.

Phoenix speaks in parables.

Halpas governs destruction through fire and war.

Malpas destroys man's thoughts and desires.

Raum is a seer concerned with theft.

Focalor has power to destroy an exorcist during the process of an exorcism.

Sabnack decays and torments man's body.

Vepar inflicts worms.

Shax destroys sight and hearing.

Vine demolishes great wall barriers and creates stormy seas.

Bifrons changes burial places of the dead bodies and lights candles on their graves.

Vual controls lust.

Hagenti turns wine into water.

Procel controls extreme hot and cold temperatures in all waters.

Furcas serves as a warrior and teacher.

Balam makes men go invisible.

Allocen is a warrior.

Caim, a seer.

Murmur controls souls of the dead.

Orobas defends the exorcist from any spirit.

Gomory controls lust.

Ose can change any mortal into any shape he wants without the person being changed aware of it.

Amy, a trader of other spirits.

Orias transforms men and gives titles.

Vapula, teacher of the sciences.

Zagan changes mortals' blood into oil and then oil into water.

Valac will deliver serpents on command.

Andras kills man at will.

Flauros will kill and mutilate.

Andrealphus changes men to birds.

Cimeries, a warrior.

Amduscias causes trees to be uprooted, crushing men.

Belial demands sacrifices.

Decarabia produces birds as familiars.

Seere speeds or slows time.

Dantalian changes man's good thoughts at will.

Andromalius causes disorder among thieves.

F. Miracle Homosexual Deliverance.[176]

I was tired of feeling distant from my husband, so on June 21, 2020, I cast out the spirits of Satan, Lucifer, and the three principalities, all on the Homosexual Deliverance List and those on the second list I had made. These are unloving and unforgiving spirits. (Rom. 1:31 NKJV). After that, I found a great difference in our relationship. I repeat this list periodically and use it in spiritual warfare.

Pastor Eloyse said these demons over homosexuality could also be battled using her list of fifty "Sexual Lust Demons."[177] She identified seven of the 80-list principalities (not Beelzebub) and the six demons from the 6-pointed star as Sexual Lust Demons. (See App. N) Park likewise faulted this star. (See Symbols and Emblems That Bring Curses chapter).

Baal and Astaroth, Isis and Osiris, and Python and Pythoness were listed in the top eight. Yeshua said to cast out the Sexual Lust Demons off children and persons who have been molested.

Pastor Eloyse said the perverse spirit and homosexuality come in through the worship of idols, inherited perversions, voyeurism, nudity, deprivation of love, neglect, abandonment as a child, different abuses, and more.[178] The numbered spirits are principalities from the 80-list in Appendix E. Pastor Eloyse also included Romans 1:18-32. Cast out these sins and their consequences along with both lists below.

- #1 Spirit of Satan, Non-responsibility for self, and evil. Spirit of Lucifer, the image of perfection, unreality, and denial.
- #9 Lucifuge Roficale, the abused person. The veil over the mind (that distorts reality).
- #8 Nebiros, exchange of spirit, networking, and codependency.
- #4 Put Satanachia, reprobate mind, hate of God, and Paranoid Schizophrenia.

Satan and Lucifer are under Python. Python is also over Satanic transference. (See the Six-Pointed Star, Symbols, Emblems that Bring Curses chapter, and Teaching on Actual Deliverance chapter).

Deliverances Added by Author

Cast these out.

The spirit of pedophilia.

Having been sexually abused at any age.

Having sexually abused anyone. Repent.

Irene Park, in The Homosexual and the Perverse Spirit, said there are three types of homosexual designs put on children, causing traits of the opposite sex. "The perverse spirit is sent forth as an agent of the spirit of divination to work a design (like a curse or spell)."

A parental design. Before the child was born child, the parents wanted a child of a different gender than the one God had given them. (Or the doctor made a mistake on the sex of the baby).

A physical design. Someone at any age is inappropriately touched or violated. This can cause them to be a prostitute, homosexual, lesbian, or bisexual.

A psychic design. A person is never touched but raped in fantasy, without knowing that the design has been worked. I believe psychic designs are entering children during drag queen story hours, and by homosexual and lesbian teachers who want them to identify with the opposite gender.

Guard your children from evil people. Cast out your own ancestral and personal curses. Cover them with the blood of Yeshua and pray for angels to protect them. Lead them in putting on their spiritual armor. (Eph. 6:10-18)

The master curse, Krodeus, is largely responsible for homosexuality, because it comes in with Put Satanachia, also named Baphomet, whom the witches and homosexuals love. Krodeus comes in by being conceived out of wedlock, with all sexual experimentation, sexual abuse, sex sins, witchcraft, secret orders and Hindu spirits. These are the reasons homosexuality is growing in every nation of the world. It may be unknown, kept secret, or obvious. (See Addendum II, Krodeus, the Bastard Curse).

Baal & Put S., #4, 80-list, are the main abusers.[179]

Isis protects secrets.[180]

Osiris. Emotionally dead males. Incest.[181]

Python (fear, imagination) and Pythoness (prostitution), Sexual Lust Demons,[181.]

Sargatanas, #7, 80-list. Defiles the spirit through sexual abuse.[182] (See App. N)

If one of the partners is masturbating or has experienced sexual abuse, there may be deprivations of intimacy within the marriage.

"Sytry procures nudity." The 80-list.

"Belial demands sacrifice." The 80-list. (See The Defilement of Women, Deliverance from Traumas chapter).

Cast out the names of the Indian tribes in your family or your state. All Scouting is built on Indian ways. Many Scouts have been molested.

Ashteroth, #3, 80-list, works with Baal and Molech. (See Satanic Ritual Abuse, Have No Other Gods chapter).

Zireck (Zurg). Self-destruction. (See Sargatanas, depression).

Read Psalm 139 if you believe lies about your identity.

Butch. Tomboy. Bisexual, Transsexual. Transvestite. Transgendered.

Hercules, an Anti-Messiah. Acting tough to be safe.[183]

Oral Sex brings a risk of cold sores.184 I have a permanent scar from cold sores; one woman got cancer in her throat from oral sex and died.

The book, It Could Have Been Me, by Jasmine Townsend.[185]

G. The Deliverance List for Familiar Spirits[186]

This is a miracle list that I first used because I was fearful when my brother sent me a letter. At the top of the list, enter the name of a person you have unforgiveness for, whom you have worshiped, whom you are afraid of, or who has abused you. Go through the list, first casting out your own faults relating to the person. Make a second copy, casting out the spirits of the other person that have come onto you. This may bring memories that you have repressed. If you believe this person abused your child, proxy or cast the person's spirits out of your child.

In July 2022, this is what Yeshua told me. I was casting out the spirits of Dr. M. and the Yokefellow leader. Because of trauma, hatred and fear are the most important to cast out. Hatred brings fear. Hatred and fear of the opposite sex bring lust.

"Perfect love casts out fear." (1 John 4:18)

When you have finished this list, go to the 80-list and cast out Agaliarept and Sargatanas, which come in from trauma. Then cast out Python, the two trinities of Satan and Lucifer. (See the Six-pointed Star, Symbols and Emblems that Bring Curses chapter).

I found this list in the Siren file. Remember to bind spirits, including Satan, Siren, and Leviathan; the prideful, hard-hearted sea monster. (Job 41). Cast out these spirits, all under Satan.

- The Spirit of (name of the person).
- Deception of
- Distortion of

Appendices

- Delusion of
- Voice control of
- Power of control of
- Rejection of
- Resentment of
- False confidence in
- Bitterness of
- Hatred of
- Rebellion of
- Break all commitments to
- Break all curses, hexes, spells, and predictions of
- Unforgiveness of
- Trespassing of
- Betrayal of
- The (false) guilt of not living up to his/her expectations.
- Servitude to
- Hypocrisy to
- Fear of
- Dread of
- Can't stand to look into his/her eyes.
- Can't stand to hear his/her voice.
- Can't stand to be in his/her presence.
- Reaction to
- Violence to
- Murder of
- Malign of
- Criticism of

- Back-biting of
- Slander of
- Intolerance of
- Bondage to commitments
- Inadequacy Spiritually

This author added the following:

- Fears from specific abusers may bring mistrust of the deliverance minister.
- The Spirit of Siren is a mermaid that lures sailors to destruction. This mermaid is the naked woman on the Starbucks cup. Naked mermaids were on a float at El Carnaval (the Mexican Mardi Gras).
- Siren and Pythoness are prostitute spirits. Use Ezekiel 23 for deliverance.
- Siren is over a living death[187]

H. Complex PTSD, Lucario

Lucario describes 12 physical or emotional symptoms of Complex PTSD that she experienced, including physical pain. This website has many chat rooms.

1. Deep Fear of Trust
2. Terminal Aloneness
3. Emotion Regulation
4. Emotional Flashbacks
5. Hypervigilance About People
6. Loss of Faith in people, the world, religion, and self
7. Profoundly Hurt Inner Child
8. Helplessness and Toxic Shame
9. Repeated Search for A Rescuer
10. Dissociation
11. Persistent Sadness and Being Suicidal
12. Muscle Armoring (which brings pain)[188]

I. More on the Jesuits

Stories of extreme persecution of believers in China and Korea, similar to the Inquisitions of Rome, have caused me to ask, did the Catholic Church start Communism? Chick published Alberto Rivera's story in booklet form in the Crusader's volumes 12 to 17.

Chiniquy warned Lincoln of the imminent assassination because of lies that Lincoln had been Catholic. Chiniquy documents that the Jesuits assassinated Lincoln, then wrote his biography to destroy his reputation and Christian testimony.[189][190]

In "Jesuits," Chick explains that Ignatius of Loyola started the Alumbrados, which became the Illuminati. He then started the Jesuits. Chick reports that the Jesuits did start modern communism. They start wars and assassinate presidents and dictators. A Jesuit helped Hitler write Mein Kampf. They wanted Jerusalem for the White Pope, so they started Islam. The Black Pope is the supreme General of the Jesuits.[191][192]

In "The Force," Chick and Alberto explain that Jesuits have brought Loyola's spiritual exercises and the behavioral sciences into the Charismatic Movement and Bible-believing churches to destroy them. But this is no reason to refuse the gift of tongues or avoid Bible-believing churches. (Mark 16:17). Chick wrote the Jesuits had spawned spiritual abominations: Freemasonry, Jehovah's Witness, Mormonism, Unity, Christian Science, and others. They also work undercover in newly formed religious bodies and secret societies.[193] (See Hindu gods, The Worship of Freemason gods, Have No Other Gods chapter).

Loyola is also said to have started the New World Order. Thirty-five groups are listed under and with the Alumbrados and the Illuminati, including the Jesuits, the Opus Dei, the United Nations, the Council on Foreign Relations, the Trilateral Commission, Freemasonry, the Bohemian club, the Bilderbergers, and the Red Cross, the modern-day version of the Knights Hospitaller, the founders of the world's hospitals. [194]

When Howard Pittman went to heaven on August 3, 1979, he counted those who died in a 15-minute period. 97.5% of them went to hell. He said only 2.5% would have gone up in the rapture, had the trumpet sounded that day. Because of false doctrines and evil abominations perpetrated by the Catholic Church, the Illuminati, the Jesuits, I believe they are largely responsible for taking many people to hell. Howard Pittman's stories are on YouTube.

Before Pastor Eloyse died in 2010, there was a regret for joining the Foursquare denomination because the Gateway District had not supported Pastor Eloyse's deliverance ministry and because the land would belong to Foursquare after her death. There was also a concern that Aimee Semple McPherson, the founder of the Foursquare church, had died at the age of 53 from an overdose of sleeping pills; this little woman kept an overwhelming schedule, holding meetings every night.[195]

Because of these concerns, I believed the Catholic Church might have started the Foursquare church. Nury Rivera, the widow of former Jesuit priest Alberto Rivera, agreed. Nury Rivera said this would put Jesuits in key positions in the Foursquare Church, as they are in many churches.

Yeshua can overcome these foundation bondages. He loves the Foursquare churches of refugees, like the one in Southeast Denver.

Many churches with "Kingdom Now" beliefs believe Yeshua has already established his kingdom and is ruling. This Catholic teaching prevents churches from teaching about the rapture. Other concerning signs in some churches is that they have no altar calls, deliverance, or spiritual warfare and few of their members read the Bible. (2 Tim. 3:5).

J. Not Being Able to Speak Up

Isis and the other goddesses that enter with infant baptism and freemasonry are enablers and are over keeping secrets. Mothers and fathers may not be able to protect their children, may abuse them or bond with or befriend a man who does. Deliver out these goddess spirits if you had infant or sprinkling baptism, freemasonry bondages, and especially if you or your ancestors were in girl scouts or any women's branch of Freemasonry. (See Goddesses Enter with Infant Baptism, Have no Other God's chapter).

After my granddaughter died in a car accident, I called my cousin's former wife, who lost her teenage daughter in a car accident. She sensed the girls in our family could not speak up. Sometimes boys can't speak up. A woman whom I met in Boston in 2012 believed I was autistic. She directed me to an online Aspie test, that showed I was half autistic and half not[196] Renounce Isis, an inherited demon, one of twenty over autism and mental illness. Deliver out the five principalities over autism; Beelzebub, Ashtaroth, Put Satanachia, Agaliarept, and Lucifuge Roficale.[197][198] (See 80-List, Appendix E).

In her chapter, "Autism and other learning difficulties," Kitchen says to renounce the curse of being treated like an animal. [199]

Parents are buying hooded jackets and hats for children with animal ears. Children's candy, cereal, and vitamins come in animal shapes. Children were dressed like animals or wore animal masks in a Noah's ark skit. Irene Park said stuffed animals carry spirits. Many children's toys have demonic themes.

The Cub Scouts ranks are Lion, Bobcat, Tiger, Wolf, Bear, and Webelos, which are all unclean animals. (Lev. 11:1-8).

Renounce and deliver out spirits of these animals, having been called animal names and believing in evolution and reincarnation.

> "But God gives it a body as He pleases, and to each seed its own body. All flesh is not the same flesh, but there is one kind of flesh of men, another flesh of animals, another of fish, and another of birds." (1 Cor. 15:38-39 NKJV)

Yeshua rebuked the deaf and dumb spirit. (Mark 9:25). (See Appendix C, More Deliverances for the Sephardic Jews).

It is easier for me to sing and pray in the spirit than in English. (1 Cor. 14:15). Renounce spiritual autism, difficulty reading the bible and praying.

I bought some books on emotions for my children when they were small. But I have found "David and I talk to God Series," based on the Bible. (See References).

Women in Ministry

Though Foursquare did not support Pastor Eloyse's deliverance ministry, it is needed in these end times. Many religious spirits silence women.

Brawner (and Whetstone) said, 1 Corinthians 14:34-35 is misused to prevent women from proclaiming the gospel. Women in Apostle Paul's time were asking their husbands during the service to explain what the speaker was saying. A better translation is: "Let you wives be quiet, for it is not permitted unto them to babble and talk in an undertone in the church; they are disturbing both the speaker and the hearers. Don't ask your husbands for explanations during the service; wait until you get home."[200] (See Rinck, Cunningham, and Whetstone, References).

In 1 Corinthians 11:10, Paul said a man needs to have his head uncovered, a woman, her head covered when they pray or prophesy. This disputes the translation of "silent" in 1 Corinthians 14:34. Both can pray and prophecy. Brawner said verse ten refers to the need to be under the anointing of the Holy Ghost, not about a hat or hair. She believes it is ok to cut one's hair but not to be shorn. (1 Cor. 11:6).

K. Spirits Over Death

Pastor Eloyse said the list of spirits in Ephesians 6:12, and all demons and evil spirits are spirits of death. Angels of death guide you to death. [201]

Psalm 88 may be used for deliverances from death spirits.

A man on the bus was having a seizure. I had some men move him to the floor, and loudly, repeatedly, rebuked the spirits of death, without naming them. The paramedics carried him out the back door without saying a word. The woman bus driver was pleased saying, "just like a woman." A few days later I saw him on the bus. He said he didn't buy his seizure medicine because he had no money.

Angels of Death.[202]

I cast these out when my niece had a brain hemorrhage. She survived but has a limitation on her speech. I proxied these, the death spirits, and a 2003 deliverance list out of my father-in-law when he had chest pain. He lived several more years and I believe, then accepted the Savior. I cast these and the death spirits out after a prolonged intestinal illness and revived!

Cast out:

Martura. Martyr. Self-sacrifice.

Masso. Acute internal anxiety. Spirit masochism.

Agrabia, over physical suffocation.

Merodach, death by cut off of communication in one's life.

Molech. The child-sacrifice (birth control, molestation, or infant baptism).

Raphael, death through physical deterioration.
    (anti-healing).

Sabnack. An angel of death under Lucifer and Merodach.[203]

Sabnack, decay and torment man's body. Aging. See 80 list.

Apollyon and Abaddon. (Rev. 9:11). [204]

Death and Suicide Spirits [205]

Zombies enter with Mormon baptism for the dead and with infant and sprinkling baptism.

Gods of death. Physical death. Tammuz. (Ezek. 8:13-14) Thanatos that attacks the brain.

Prince of Death. Beelzebub.

Death of the emotions. Osiris and Tammuz.

Spiritual death. Osiris, Sargatanas (see 80-list), Zombies.

Worship of death. Osiris.

Protectress of the dead. Isis.

Living death. Siren.

Death as an act of the will. Suicide. Put Satanachia. (See 80-list).

Self-Death. Beelzebub.

Death wish. Enyo and Oblivio. The death wish is over all curses. It is housed in and attacks the brain. This can include the wish for someone else to die. [206]

Zeus. [207]

Murder Spirits

Satan, (John 10:10) and Lucifer, (Is. 14:12-20). (See Miracle Homosexual Deliverance, Appendix F and the Six-pointed Star, Symbols and Emblems that Bring Curses chapter).

Andras, kills man at will.

Flauros, will kill and mutilate.

Glasyalabolas, homicide, bloodshed.

Fleurety, over war.

All but Lucifer are from the 80-list.

Appendix L.
American Indian deliverances CLF 121374

Parenthesis are added by author.

Idolatry of all below: (Inherited, active, repressed, dormant, (hidden) CLF)

Navajo, Cherokee, and all tribes.

Lust for Indian artifacts. Archaeology.

Rings, jewelry, turquoise, coral.

Thunderbirds. Totem Poles, Pictures.

War shields, weapons. (Tomahawks, hatchets, drums)

(War shields, medicine wheels, & dream catchers, are similar)

Arrowheads, dances, chants.

Headdresses: fur, feathers (eagle), animal heads, teeth, claws.

Leather bags of fetishes, feathers, beads.

Irene Park said that witches and indians use feathers as a fetish.

Amulets (including bear claws). Braids and bear grease.

Sand paintings. Idolatry of buffaloes.

Idolatry of endurance, torture, and suffering. (In the initiations in the Boy Scout Order of Arrow & the Kiva Lodge, as a rite of passage)

Of dwellings: Tepees, Museums. Fascination with ruins.

Idolatry of Indian culture

Songs. History. Indian rugs, weavings, horses, pintos.

War paint. Masks. Bells. Wind bells. Pottery. Nudity. Hair.

God's eyes. Bartering. Ceremonies. Peace pipes.

Saddles, leather jackets, belts, Buckskin, Moccasins.

(Irene Park said the stars or asterisk buttons on moccasins are symbols for hexes)

White (birch) bark Canoes. Indian romance.

Burial grounds. (Irene Park danced nude)

Hunting grounds in the sky. (A lie; where deceased warriors go)

Indian women: Hiawatha. Evangeline. Pocahontas.

Indian men: Crazy horse. Sitting Bull.

Medicine men. Shamans. Witchcraft.

Herbs, potions, peyote, cactus, mushrooms.

(Using Satan to heal can bring a worse illness like cancer)

Trances and spell casting.

Scalping. (Necessary for induction as a warrior)

Indian Infirmities/Bondages

Insanity, delirium, diabetes, alcoholism, schizophrenia.

(Homosexuality & Lesbianism. Irene A. Park, The Witch that Switched)

(Most significant bondages)

The Krodeus curses, sin and destruction. Ex. 20, Lev. 27-28.

Groves (the woods). Sodomites. 1 Kings 14:23-24.

Indian Dances. Fear. Terror.

Children die or are rejected. 1 Kings 11:7. CLF Molech pattern.

Irene A. Park, Witchcraft Idolatry and Indian Ways, cdmin.com

Gene Moody Deliverance Manual. Indian curse list.

Appendix M.

Deliverance from Spirits of Indigenous peoples

Be like Joseph. Get delivered from and forgive what has terrorized you. Become an advocate for deliverance to heal and draw others to Yeshua,

"But as for you, you meant evil against me; but God meant it for good, in order to bring it about as it is this day, to save many people alive." (Gen. 50:20)

"None of them shall teach his neighbor, and none his brother, saying, 'Know the LORD,' for all shall know Me, from the least of them to the greatest of them." (Heb. 8:11)

Horrors from Canada

Dr. Meri Crouley and Kevin Annett have exposed the ritual killing by rich and powerful people of Indian children who attended residential schools in Canada. Her book: Freedom Cry: Women Fighting Trafficking. September 30th is the annual National Day for Truth and Reconciliation in Canada regarding this horror.

The United States of America

Visiting Rexa in the nursing home, I met Elizabeth who said her grandpa was the first missionary to the Navajos in New Mexico. 500 children came to a school auditorium for Sunday school.

From Mexico

The worship of Olmec heads, from the Yucatan Peninsula. This cult preceded the Aztecs and Mayans, originated from African ancestors, and involved human sacrifice. My father-in law and his neighbor created a Styrofoam Olmec god covered with plaster for his new atrium.

In Denver, 2007. Jordan said he was saved as I witnessed on the bus 6 years prior. He said his family from the Yucatan, several generations ago, quit worshiping the Mayan Baal god named "Menhenkinsin."

I learned from the August 2007 San Carlos Times, the Yaki or Yaqui Indians from Obregon return every year during Semana Santa to appease the rain god, Yuku, who they believe, with his wife, live on Cerros las Tetas de Cabra, the sacred twin peaks mountain. The ceremonies are believed to prevent starvation, drought and the sinking of ships at sea. These actually involve the sacrifice of children.

The Pipil Tribe from El Salvador settled in central Mexico. They were one of the few tribes to abolish human sacrifice.

My Anthropology professor said American corporations got the poor landowners drunk, bought their land, fenced it in and grew corn, making high fructose corn syrup.

The legend of Llorona, that she drowned her children and herself in a river, may still be used to terrify children into obedience.

The Seri Indians of Senora were fierce fighters, swift runners, fishermen, and were said to have been cannibalistic.

The Zapatistas of Chiapas have oppressed those who left a mixture of Catholicism and indigenous practices. Voice of the Martyrs put the state on their world map. Islam has moved in with a school for children.

Aztec and Other Gods

Tlāloc, the rain god. Quetzalcoatl, the creator god, is depicted by a serpent that gave corn and arts to humans. The people are dependent on human sacrifices to the gods at the summit of a pyramid. Rocky Mtn News, Dec. 6, 1992.

Guide Spirits. #4, CLF.

The god, Mesapotyl, demands sacrifices of babies, virgins and mothers. The antichrist lives in the pyramids and will fight the Ancient of Days.

The spirits of a former dictator are still in control.

Zebreius, fights believers with a spell.

Antonius attacks love.

Entellectus deceives.

A person with Blackfoot Indian ancestry. CLF 072874.

1/32 ancestry is Indian. They received deliverance from: Schizophrenia, sexual perversion., sexual modification, sexual frigidity, fear, revenge, retaliation, attempted murder.

Agabus. A personal guardian guide brought obesity, financial and physical destruction. Grounds, Indian ancestry, insecurity, and rejection. Worshiping gods of fertility and food.

Tanus CLF 102780

Tanning of hides. Opens up for persecution and anguish for being an American Indian. Passivity. Fantasy of American Indians.

A squaw spirit. Women are used and do all the dirty work. Men hunt and ride horses or motorcycles.

Cherokee Ancestry in a woman. 092977

To save a child, oaths are made to the sun. But someone dies anyway.

A wolf trail leads from earth and heaven (at time of death).

She said scalps of women are more sought after than those of men.

She spoke of Lesbianism, of the fear of being raped, and said the reaction to rejection is to be helpless, dependent, and weak.

The Sun Dance Ceremony

A muchacho fasts 5 days before this rite of passage initiation when he will become a man.

This woman seemed to indicate that women also participate in this ceremony and may become a sacrifice, dying because of the torture.

In about 2007, I met a man and his wife from South Dakota with Indian ancestry, on the bus. They were without housing for a few days. I had posted a list at CLF and was able to find housing for them. He said some of his relatives, but not himself, had participated in this initiation ceremony.

Britanica speaks of this ceremony being outlawed for many years in the United States and Canada. In this ceremony, training the muchacho to be a warrior, articles are inserted under the skin of the back to test endurance. The youth pulls a load or is hung from the ceiling of the Kiva lodge, with these insertions in his back. I saw a similar torture practiced in East India on Saturday morning Christian TV.

I believe the Order of the Arrow 24-hour initiation is patterned after this ceremony. Hard work, no food, not able to speak, sleeping alone in the woods, nudity. Only wearing a loincloth and a vest my husband had to make himself from leather. Apache Warriors, by Netzley, Kidhaven Press, verifies the Order of the Arrow is similar to Apache warrior training.

South America and Nicaragua, The Jesuits Expelled

Literacy and income are higher near the former Jesuit missions that thrived until 1767, when King Charles III of Spain expelled all Jesuits from the Spanish Empire. Stone ruins are visible in South America.

Reuters reported "Nicaragua cancels legal status of Catholic Jesuit order," August 23, 2023.

Appendix N

Sexual Lust Demons

Eloyse Ephraim Badgett, "Sexual Lust Demons," Handbook for Strategic Level Spiritual Warfare for the Middle East and Europe (Lakewood, CO: Lakewood Foursquare Church/ Christian Living Fellowship, 1996), 6.1 -6.8.

80 = from the 80 list. See Appendix E. [Added by author].

1. Baal. Idolatry of the phallus, males, and sex life, romantic love, father power, male aggression, compulsions. 80.

2. Astaroth (Astarte). Idolatry of fertility, females, and sex life, mother power, seduction (subconscious), wooing, compromise. 80.

3. Isis. Protectress of the dead, rests in female reproductive system, inherited sex perversion (drives and practices).

4. Sytry. Procures nudity. 80.

5. Osiris. "The dead," incest, "dead males" (autistic male society) and mostly the thing alive is the phallus (penis) and it is worshiped. Emotional death (or deaths) stimulates redirected emotions into sex drives.

6. Beleth. A vicious entity, controls lust. 80.

7. Python. Imagination, secret thoughts, subconscious messages , faith in Satan (Fear), convincing power, spiritual reception, hypnotic spell.

8. Pythoness. Harlotry, prostitution, seduction (imagined or actual), divination.

9. Put Satanachia. Has grounds through guilt from past sex life including masturbation, fantasizing and exposure, etc. A Perverse spirit, causes incest, sodomy, lesbianism, homosexuality, fornication and adultery. Practices psychic marriages. 80.

10. Fleurety. puts lust in mankind's mind. 80.

11. Sargatanas. Enters into a person's secret thoughts, creates a cool platonic marriage relationship, but no real spirit-exchange (bonding). Through sexual abuse, incest, and molestation (defiles the spirit). Fornication, adultery, self-incest, masturbation, sexual violations in (or out of) marriage bed. 80.

Appendices

12. Eligor. Causes war and lust. 80.

13. Semarimis. The lust to get something for the "self." Deep subliminal desires that rule through subconscious inadequacy, psychic powers, communion with the dead, idolatry of love.

14. Janus. The "I" of personal exclusiveness which causes the two faces (dependent-independent) or masks to manifest. Creates actor/actress personality, that causes one to flirt and draw attention to self.

15. Saleos. Controls lust. 80.

16. Hedone. Lust for pleasurable experiences.

17. Lucius. Unfulfilled love, non-reciprocal love, over-extension of love, self-rebellion (turning and betraying one's own spirit-man).

18. Vual. Controls lust. 80.

19. Gomory. Controls lust. 80.

20. Sabean. (Lives in the spleen and bowels) inherited hate, creative hate, reverse activity (in the spleen and bowels) of hate pouring forth instead of love. Thus, using hate as a motivating power, it generates lust (imitation of love); a drive to be accepted. The grounds can be prenatal hatred of father. Cats.

21. Lucifer. (The serpent in the Garden of Eden, the hiss, the magic spell, the hunger for knowledge, the desire for power, magic). An angel of light, light-bringer, day star, self-beauty, self-exaltation, spiritual-deception, mysticism, self-aggrandizement, egocentricity, idolatry of the spiritual, lime-lighting, attention-getting, salesmanship, showmanship, demanding to be heard. "I will be." "I am." Whatever one's concept of love is, that is one's concept of self. (Self-identity). "I am special because ...."

22. Raphael. Too much life, over-reacting, exotic condition.

23. Pan. Subconscious morbid fears, masturbation, intimidation, mood-music (of all kinds, including "rock" & "rap"). Dreams.

24. Eve. Inherited emotional dependency on males (in women).

25. Tammuz. Subconscious dependency, worship of babies and children, Messiah complex, demonic self-deprivation, sado-masochism.

26. Nimrod. (Subliminal will-to-power) Power of rejection and judgment, subconscious hate toward God, insecurity, non-communication, non-reconciliation, confusion, self-works, sadism, idolatry, humanism, subconscious wall of hate between others and self, inner rebellion, misappropriation of love.

27. Agaliarept. (Located in the reproductive system) A prediction of LIES. Predictions of past or future. Creates animosity, impending doom, a foreboding, catastrophes and tragedies. A delusion demon (paranoia). Surfaces at night and expresses fears. Breaks interpersonal relationships. Blocks faith. Out of fear, it peers into the future and predicts. Triggers imagination.

Located in the womb or prostate gland (houses of fear) it transfers fear from the reproductive system to the tail bone and up the spinal column and transfers it into a yearning For Love.

Idolatry of authority figures (usually males). Locks up the spirit, through fear-of-rejection [by] a male image. Because one loves the male, one wants to believe him. [Grounds, sexual abuse. Cancer]. 80.

28. Lucifuge Roficale. [The dragon of death]. The veil that distorts reality. An attitude of idolatry. He defames spiritual leaders and sets them up for a downfall. Defensiveness.

He is caused by subconscious anger at others, subconscious unforgiveness of others, unconscious hatred of God from being battered, either physically, emotionally, or mentally. Rejection of one's own nationality. Sorrow of heart. Deep spirit grieving. Subconscious weeping, chronic anxiety. Weakness testing for strength.

He creates a crust of idolatry around one's spirit-man that keeps love out. This in turn sets a person to receive an imitation of love called lust. 80.

29. Rapha. Unreality.
30. Ra, Re, or Phra. Sado-masochism.
31. Lammea. Broken close relationships.
32. Chelsea. Inherited desire to display one's body.
33. Cybele. Inherited mysticism, rejection of femininity.
34. Gaea. Inherited earthly-mindedness (carnality).
35. Rema. Inherited rejection; seeking acceptance.
36. Nymph. Inherited uncontrollable sex passions.
37. Tantalis. In males, tantalizing women.
38. (Titaness) Succubi. Nightmare, a female demon who lies with sleeping men and seeks to have sexual intercourse.
39. (Titan) Incubi. Nightmare, a male demon or spirit who lies with sleeping women and seeks to have sexual intercourse. [It seemed right to reverse Titan and Titaness].
40. Rhea. a mother spirit in women often seeks men to mother.
41. Venus. Goddess of love (spring bloom and beauty).
42. Cupid. God of desire, longing and passion (a naked winged boy).

43. Aphrodite. Goddess of love (of sea foam born), especially beautiful. (Mental retardation. Grounds, sexual or inherited sexual misconduct. Anna's A -Z list).
44. Mercury. (Hermes. Messenger of Zeus). An athletic god with a lithe, graceful body. A lover; inspires melodious speech and eloquence.
45. Hermaphrodite. Shy youth (brought up by nymphs). A single body with both male and female sexes.
46. Juno. Goddess of marriage.
47. Minerva. Goddess of wisdom.
48. Eros. God of passionate love. (Erotic, the sensual, passionate love of men and women).
49. Apollo. God of divine radiance (present wherever there is light). Intellectualism, as separated from the true emotions of one's spirit (backed by God).

Appendix O

Postpartum Depression

Dr. William Sears lists 7 reasons for Postpartum depression.

#1 A previous History of depression or difficulty coping with combined stresses.

#2 Exchanging a high-status career for motherhood. ...

#3 An unwanted pregnancy. ...

#4 Marital discord.

#5 A negative birth experience in which fear and pain predominate.

#6 An ill or premature baby.

#7 Is any situation that separates mother and baby and interferes with a close mother-infant attachment shortly after birth. (Like being in an incubator or with strict schedule feeding).

We students in nursing school were instructed in a "change theory," possibly "Lewin's Nursing Theory of Change." We were to tell the new mothers to feed their babies only every four hours.

A "change theory" seems to have been used after 9/11 and during COVID-19 so that people gave up their freedoms. These can be compared to the use of lies in "brain washing."

Warning signs Sears lists are: insomnia, loss of appetite, unfounded nagging, less attention to grooming, and not wanting to get out of the house. Sears said others should do the housework and care for older children. Limit visitors, avoid isolation, get exercise and a eat a balanced diet. He recommends a Le Leche League support group. https://lllusa.org This website is in Spanish and English. (See Parenting, in References).

I believe Sears numbers: 3, 4, and 7, moving to Nebraska along with the death of her father three months before I was born, and a trauma, combined to give my mother postpartum psychosis. She stayed in bed and was beating us 2 older children. (See My Story, page 19).

Dr. William Sears, and Dr. James Dobson on Family Talk radio broadcasts, are instructing adults to act with love towards children instead of a conditioning and withdrawal of love, that breeds rebellion and hatred. Discipline should be lovingly administered immediately after willful defiance, not over spilled milk. (Prov. 13:24, 22:6). If you are unmercifully beating your child, get delivered from witchcraft spirits. This can be hidden or overt.

Pastor Eloyse said parents must have a right relationship, use their will in love, to bring holiness at the time of conception. Satan would have the will repressed, blocked. Then everything becomes distorted, unreal. May 16, 1976. (See 80-list, App. E. Repression, See Sex Trafficking Addendum)

Cast out:
   Fears. (See Zombie, Have No Other Gods chapter).
   Depression, #7, Appendix E.
   The spirits of death, Appendix K.
   Get prayer and medical help!
   There is a free and confidential hotline 24 hours a day, 7 days a week for pregnant moms and new moms, in English and Spanish.
   The National Maternal Mental Health Hotline can help. Call or send a text message to 1-833-TLC-MAMA (1-833-852-6262).
   988 is the suicide and crisis lifeline.
   Dr. William Sears, Parenting and Childcare A guide for Christian Parents (Nashville: Thomas Nelson 1993), 106 – 110

Endnotes

1. Dr. Richard Kent. "Dr. Maurice Rawlings Explains Near Death Experiences," Free Christian Teaching TV. Freely you have received, freely give – Matthew 10:8

2. Tom Horn Mar 8, 2020 https://www.youtube.com/watch?v=Goq8vYzLno4 (September 9, 2021). Thomas Horn, The Wormwood Prophecy (Lake Mary, FL: Charisma House 2019), 27.

3. An Extremely Brazen Opening Ceremony to the Commonwealth Games This Year, Openly Worshipping Baal, August 2, 2022. Australian National Review https://www.australiannationalreview.com/lifestyle/an-extremely-brazen-opening-ceremony-to-the-commonwealth-games-this-year-openly-worshipping-baal/ (August 4, 2022).

4. Oliveira. "4 HOURS Brother Carlos *Casting Out Your Demons.*"

5. David El-Cana Bryan, *The Serpent and the Savior*, (Monee, IL, 2022). Church of Glad Tidings, Live Oak, CA 530.671.3160 https://churchofgladtidings.com/

6. Fernando Perez. "1 Hour of Powerful Spiritual Warfare Prayer Against Curses and Demons." https://www.youtube.com/watch?v=AnY9qakBYBA

7. Lew White, *Fossilized Customs, The Pagan Origins of Popular Customs*, Ninth Ed. (Louisville: Torah Zone, 2010). 198-199, 201.

8   Gordon Robertson, "The Seat of Satan: Ancient Pergamum." https://www1.cbn.com/700club/seat-satan-ancient-pergamum (September 19, 2020)

9   Gordon Robertson, "The Seat of Satan: Nazi Germany." https://www1.cbn.com/700club/seat-satan-nazi-germany (September 19, 2020)

10 V. Patrick Johnstone, *Operation World* (Grand Rapids: Zondervan 5th ed 1993) 575.

11 Judith Herman, MD. *Trauma and Recovery* (New York City: Basic Books, Harper Collins, 1997), 113. E.H. Carmen, P.P. Ricker, and T. Mills. "Victims of Violence and Psychiatric Illness," American Journal of Psychiatruy141 (1984): 378-83.

12 Pastor Thomas Fritch, "How to win souls to Christ." CLF summer camp, June 23 to 27, 1986, The Mountain Center, 32689 Hwy. 40, Evergreen, CO 80439.

13 William Fay, "How to Share the Gospel Without an Argument," August 1996, Pastor Steve Caroll, Arvada Central Baptist, Arvada CO. http://www.sharejesuswithoutfear.com/

14 Dr. Rebecca Brown, *He Came to Set the Captives Free*. (Chino, CA. Chick Publications, 1986), 8-9.

15 Brown, *He Came to Set the Captives Free*, 83-135.

16 Sanchez, Dell F Ph.D. *The Last Exodus,* El Ultimo Exodus, (San Antonio: Jubilee Alive Books, 1998), 42

17 Sid Roth's It's Supernatural Guest: Dell Sanchez September 14, 2004.

18 Sanchez, *The Last Exodus*, 20.

19 Encarta 97 Encyclopedia, Microsoft 1995, Illustration N, 90.

19 Dell F. Sanchez, Ph.D. The *Last Exodus*, (San Antonio: Jubilee Alive Books, 1998), 88-90.

Endnotes

20 Sanchez, *The Last Exodus*, 63-68.

21 Paul Johnson, *A History of the Jews* (New York: Harper Perennial, 1987), 226.

22 Dell F. Sanchez Ph.D. "Learn More, Discover your Jewish Heritage." American Anusim - Restoring Anusim Identity: https://americananusim.org/learn-more-1 (September 20, 2020).

23 Jason Mandryk. *"Operation World."* (Colorado Springs: Biblica 2010), 866.

24 Nury S. Rivera, Iglesia Baluarte de la Fe, Jacksonville, FL. nuryriveramci@yahoo.com

25 Visión en Acción Misión Rescate, Vision in Action Mental Health Sanctuary, near Juarez, Mexico. viamhs.org

26 Dr. Dell F. Sanchez, *Curse of the Inquisition: Not Cursed but Blessed!* 1 part DVD. https://americananusim.org

27 Robert Lowry, "What can wash away my sin" (1876). https://hymnary.org/tune/what_can_wash_away_my_sin_lowry (January 14, 2021).

28 H. A. Baker, *Vision Beyond the Veil*, 10th ed. (Minneapolis: Osterhus). 69.

29 theythoughtforthemselves.com Click 'FREE". Then click to 'order' or to 'read' in Russian, Hebrew, or English. 5 Evangelical copies of this book, $5.00 plus postage. Sid Roth Partner Services 704-943-6500.

29 Sid Roth, It's Supernatural! & Messianic Vision P. O. Box 39222. Charlotte, NC 28278.

30 Irene A. Park, *Witchcraft, Puppets, and Voodoo.* (New Port Richey: Irene Park Ministries, 1983). 11-13. 7 booklets available in PDF from pastorherb@cdmin.com.

31 Samuele Bacchiocchi, *From Sabbath to Sunday*, A historical Investigation of the Rise of Sunday Observance in Early Christianity. (Rome: Pontifical Gregorian University Press 1977), 311

32 David Holmgren, teacher of Messianic Studies, World Ministries International, Stanwood, WA. 44.

33 Jonathan H. Hansen, *"Warning" The Church Has Divorced Itself From Its Roots.* (Stanwood, WA.: Valley Press, 2000) 44.

33 Hansen, *"Warning"*, 46.

34 "The Most Astonishing Chromosome Count Ever!" So Greatly Loved, Sogreatlyloved December 18, 2019 https://sogreatlyoved.blog/2019/12/18/the-most-astonishing-chromosome-count-ever/

34 Mary Nell on Ron Wyatt and the Ark of the Covenant REVISED Apr 13, 2021, ronwyatt.com https://www.youtube.com/watch?v=6Azzg6BSw_4 (May 5, 2022).

35 Irene A. Park. *"Modernized Paganism"* (Freemasonry) (New Port Richey: Irene Park Ministries, 1982), 3.

36 Irene A. Park, *The Witch that Switched*, (New Port Richey: Christ's Deliverance Ministries, Inc., 1980). 77

37 Glen and Erma Miller, "Whence Came St. Valentine's Day" (Hot Springs, AR: Lake Hamilton Bible Camp, 1988), 3, 7.

38 Carla Butaud, *"The "It" Factor,"* Lake Hamilton Bible Camp Online, 11-26-16.

39 Eloyse Ephraim Badgett, *"Krodeus deliverance pattern."* CLF, 1978.

40 Eloyse Ephraim Badgett, *"Krodeus ministry."* Halloween. CLF. July 15, 1976.

41 Rev. Alexander Hislop, *The Two Babylons or the Papal Worship* (Neptune, NJ: Loizeaux Bro., 1959), 160-164.

42 Hislop, *The Two Babylons*, 91.

43 Merrill, F. Unger, *Unger's Bible Dictionary* (Chicago: Moody Press, 1966), 412.

44 Cynthia Gorney, *"A People Apart,"* National Geographic." Nov. 2008, 78-101.

45 "Justus's Ritual Calendar" (Parker, CO: Justus Unlimited Inc. 1991).

46 Dr. Rebecca Brown, *He Came to Set the Captives Free.* (Chino, CA. Chick Publications, 1986), 68-74.

47 Irene A. Park, *The Witch that Switched*, (New Port Richey: Christ's Deliverance Ministries, Inc., 1980). 77.

48 Irene A. Park, *Seven Pagan High Masses and Halloween* (New Port Richey: Irene Park Ministries Inc., 1982), 3, 4, 9, 10.

49 Thomas R. Horn. Josh Peck (Director) *"Silent Cry: The Darker Side of Trafficking,"* September 25, 2020. Amazon. https://www.amazon.com/Silent-Cry-Darker-Side-Trafficking/dp/B08JLXYN56 (December 16, 2020).

50 Silent Cry: *"The Conspiracy That is True."* October 11, 2020, https://subsplash.com/skywatchtv/lb/mi/+45736vd (December 16, 2020).

51 Rebecca Brown, MD., *Prepare for War.* (New Kensington, PA: Whitaker 1987), 215.

52 *Prepare for War*, 219-222.

53 Nancy Stimson, "Voluntary Climbing Ban In June," May 24, 2013, National Park Service, https://www.nps.gov/deto/learn/news/voluntary-climbing-ban-at-devils-tower-in-june.htm

54 Pastor Eloyse Badgett, *"Nimrod, A Power Demon,"* unpublished work CLF, 3-19-79.

55 Pastor Eloyse Badgett, *"Molech Deliverance Pattern,"* CLF.

56 H. B. Hayes, *"Developing Unborn Baby at 8 Weeks,"* Heritage House, 919 S. Main ST, Snowflake, AZ 85937. www.hh76.org. 1-800-858-3040.

57 Tom Horn & Cris Putnam, Petrus Romanus, *The Final Pope is Here* (Crane, MO: Defender. 2012), 312-319.

58 Rexa Daniels, *"Micah, Treasures of Wickedness. Deliverance from Demons Associated with Riches and Wealth."* Unpublished work CLF.

59 Ralph Edward Woodrow, *Babylon Mystery Religion Ancient and Modern* (Riverside: Ralph Woodrow Evangelistic Assn, Inc. 1993), 44.

60 Woodrow, *Babylon Mystery*, 21-22.

61 Pastor Eloyse Badgett, *"Infant baptism Zombie/Zeus deliverance pattern,"* CLF.

62 Anna Paraseah, *Zombie, A-Z demon names*. Unpublished manuscript. Lakewood, CO: Be Free, 2006.

63 Jim Landry, *Judging Your Parents*, *"The Hidden Sin"* (Beaumon3t, TX: In Jesus Name 2004), 20, 21.

64 Anna Paraseah, death spirits, *A – Z dictionary*, unpublished manuscript Lakewood, Co Be Free.

65 Orloue Gisselquist. *Called to Preach, The Life and Ministry of Rev. J.O. Gisselquist*, 1888-1968 (Orloue N. Gisselquist 1999), 90.

66 Herbert Mjorud, *Your Authority to Believe* (Carol Stream IL: Creation House, 1975), 90.

67 Ralph Edward Woodrow, *Babylon Mystery Religion Ancient and Modern* (Riverside: Ralph Woodrow Evangelistic Assn, Inc. 1993), 7-22.

68 Jack T. Chick, "Are Roman Catholics Christians?" (Jack T. Chick LLC. 1985) 20. www.chick.com

69 Chick, "Are Roman Catholics," 10.

70 Rev. Alexander Hislop, *The Two Babylons or the Papal Worship* (Neptune, NJ: Loizeaux Bro., 1959), 164.

Endnotes

71 *"The Society of Jesus."* Wikipedia the Free Encyclopedia. wikipedia.org/wiki/Society_of_Jesus (January 16, 2019).

72 Jack T. Chick, *Double-Cross, the Crusaders,* Alberto part two, vol. 13 (Chino: Chick Publications, 1981), 14.

73 Henry H. Halley, *Pocket Bible Handbook* 19h ed. rev. (Chicago: Henry H. Halley, 1951), 689.

74 Ron Campbell, "Unearthing the Mysteries of Masonry," Charisma (November 1997), 74.

75 Campbell, *"Unearthing the Mysteries,"* 73, 76, 115.

76 Selwyn Stevens Ph.D., *Unmasking Freemasonry, Removing the Hoodwink* (Wellington, N Z: Jubilee Resources, 2007), 29.

77 Yvonne Kitchen, *Freemasonry Death in The Family* (Mountain Gate, Victoria: Fruitful Vine, 1997), 67-72. media@fruitfulvine.org

78 Stevens, *Unmasking Freemasonry,* 8.

79 Stevens, *Unmasking Freemasonry,* 13.

80 Stevens, *Unmasking Freemasonry,* 28.

81 Open Line, June 19, 2001. www.moodyaudio.com.

82 Seek Partners International Inc. Support - Enlighten - Equip - Kingdom https://seekpartners.org/people

83 Irene A. Park. *Modernized Paganism* (on Freemasonry) (New Port Richey: Irene Park Ministries, 1982), 1.

84 C. Todd Lopez *"Male hazing most common type of sexual assault, expert reveals."* WASHINGTON (Army News Service, April 11, 2016). https://www.army.mil/article/166188/male_hazing_most_common_type_of_sexual_assault_expert_reveals (December 22, 2021).

85 Pointman International Ministries - Home https://www.pmim.org. 1-800-877-8387

86 Earl Davis, "Demonbuster.com Deliverance Manual." http://demonbuster.com/war.html (June 17, 2020).

87 Irene A. Park, *Witchcraft Idolatry and Indian Ways* (New Port Richey: Irene Park Ministries, 1982), 7.

88 Park, *Indian Ways*, 4, 22, 27.

89 Park, *Indian Ways*, 7, 8.

90 Jim Landry, *Orishas African Hidden Gods of Worship*, (Jacksonville, IL: Truth Book, 2016).

91 Irene A. Park, *What Every Christian Should know about Symbols, Signs, and Emblems*, (New Port Richey: Irene Park Ministries, 1982). pastorherb@cdmin.com.

92 Irene A. Park, *Witchcraft Idolatry and Indian Ways* (New Port Richey: Irene Park Ministries, 1982), 27.

93 Jack T. Chick, *Double-Cross, the Crusaders, Alberto part two*, vol. 13, (Chino: Chick Publications, 1981), 7.

94 Eloyse Ephraim Badgett, *"Tammuz Teaching."* CLF 1-23-79. January 23, 1979.

95 Eloyse Ephraim Badgett, Python Pattern, *"Power over Israel."* Handbook for Strategic Level Spiritual Warfare for the Middle East and Europe (Lakewood, CO: Lakewood Foursquare Church/Christian Living Fellowship, 1996), 7.1 - 7.8.

96 Irene A. Park, *Modernized Paganism*, (New Port Richey: Irene Park Ministries, 1982). 8. pastorherb@cdmin.com.

97 Dr. O.J. Graham, The Six-Pointed Star, Lectures August 16, 1999, https://www.masoniclibrary.org.au/research/list-lectures/176--the-six-pointed-star.html

98 O.J. Graham, The Six-Pointed Star, 4th ed. (Don Mills, Ontario: Free Press, 2000), 123-130. www.OJGraham.com.

Endnotes

99 Eloyse Ephraim Badgett. *"Satanic Transfer,"* CLF, December 15, 2005.

100 Pastor Eloyse Badgett. *"Do demons have proper names?"* Cassette. CLF.

101 Merrill, F. Unger, *Unger's Bible Dictionary* (Chicago: Moody Press, 1966), 411-418.

102 Pastor Hector Soberanis, Horeb El Monte De Dios, 11111 E Mississippi Ave, Aurora STE 100, Colorado 80012.

103 Gary Whetstone, *Conquering Your Unseen Enemies.* (New Castle, DE: Gary Whetstone. 1999), 7 - 26.

104 Lisa Bevere, *Kissed the Girls and Made Them Cry* (Nashville: Thomas Nelson 2002), 8.

105 Micah Stephen Bell, *No Other Gods* 6th ed. (Euless, TX: Key Ministries, 2002), 18.

106 Pastor Eloyse Badgett, Anti-Health List 1 and 2, CLF.

107 Pastor Eloyse Badgett, *"Put Satanachia Pattern,"* CLF, April 12, 1978.

108 Irene A. Park, *"Witchcraft, Puppets, and Voodoo."* (New Port Richey: Irene Park Ministries, 1983), 5. pastorherb@cdmin.com.

109 Yvonne Kitchen, *Freemasonry Death in The Family.* (Mountain Gate, Victoria: Fruitful Vine, 1997), 53. media@fruitfulvine.org

110 Meridel Rawlings Ph.D., *Stain Remover: Healing the Indelible Stain of Child Sexual Abuse* (Mevasseret Zion, Israel: Still Small Voice, 2021), 159, 160. https://stillsmallvoice.tv Email: meridel.rawlings@gmail.com

111 Gene & Earline Moody, *"87LHCD7-9 - Gene & Earline Moody"* Lake Hamilton.org http://lhbconline.com/gene-earline-moody/ (February 12, 2020)

112 Mina R. Brawner, MD., *Woman in the Word* (Dallas: Christ for the Nations, 1975), 34-35.

113 Irene A. Park, *"Witchcraft, Puppets, and Voodoo."* (New Port Richey: Irene Park Ministries, 1983). 4.

114 Anna Paraseah. *"Death Spirits."* A-Z Dictionary. CLF.

115 Yvonne Kitchen, *Freemasonry Death in The Family.* (Mountain Gate, Victoria: Fruitful Vine, 1997), 20 -22. media@fruitfulvine.org

116 Lilly Hope Lucario, *"12 Life-Impacting Symptoms Complex PTSD Survivors Endure,"* August 17, 2017, https://themighty.com/2017/08/life-impacting-symptoms-of-complex-post-traumatic-stress-disorder-ptsd/

117 Ruth S. Olson, "COVID-19 Deliverance," http://givingyeshua.com

118 Anna Paraseah, A-Z Dictionary. CLF.

119 Pastor Eloyse Badgett, *"Nimrod, A power demon,"* CLF, March 19, 1979.

120 Eloyse Ephraim Badgett, *"Sexual Lust Demons,"* "Handbook for Strategic Level Spiritual Warfare for the Middle East and Europe (Lakewood, CO: Lakewood Foursquare Church/Christian Living Fellowship, 1996), Nimrod. 6.5.

121 Badgett, *"Handbook,* Sabean. CLF. 6.4.

122 Paul Johnson, *A History of the Jews* (New York: Harper Perennial, 1987), 515. 516

123 Eric Metaxis, Bonhoeffer: *Pastor, Martyr, Prophet, Spy* (Nashville: Thomas Nelson, 2010), 93-94.

124 Pastor Eloyse Badgett, *"Tython, - Typhon,"* CLF, February 28, 1978.

125 Eloyse Ephraim Badgett, *"Typhon deliverance pattern."* CLF, February 27, 1978.

126 Yvonne Kitchen, *Freemasonry Death in The Family.* (Mountain Gate, Victoria: Fruitful Vine, 1997), 137. media@fruitfulvine.org

127 Pastor Eloyse Badgett, *"Angels of Death."* CLF, July 23, 1988.

128 Jack T. Chick, "Are Roman Catholics Christians?" (Chino: Jack T. Chick LLC. 1985), 6. https://www.chick.com/products/tract?stk=71

129 Jack T. Chick, *Angel of Light*. (Chino: Jack T. Chick LLC. 1978).

130 Charles Chiniquy, *The Priest, the Woman, and the Confessional* (Chino: Jack T. Chick LLC. Public domain)

131 Charles Chiniquy, Priest, Woman & Confessional. https://www.gutenberg.org/files/20120/20120-h/20120-h.htm (March 15, 2021)

132 Judith Herman, MD. *Trauma and Recovery* (New York City: Basic Books, Harper Collins, 1997), 119

133 Melinda Beck, Karen Springen, and Donna Foote. "Sex and Psychotherapy: A current Affair." Newsweek April 13, 1992: 55.

134 Beck, Sex and Psychotherapy: 54.

135 Christine P. Bartholomew. "Pope ends a secrecy rule for Catholic sexual abuse cases, but many barriers to justice remain for victims." January 13, 2020. https://theconversation.com/pope-ends-a-secrecy-rule-for-catholic-sexual-abuse-cases-but-for-victims-many-barriers-to-justice-remain-129434

136 Tom Horn, and Cris Putnam. Petrus Romanus, *the Final Pope, is Here* (Crane, MO: Defender. 2012), 221, 222.

137 James Brundage, *Law, Sex, and Christianity in Medieval Europe* (University of Chicago Press, 1990), 473.

138 Mary Annette Pember "Trauma May Be Woven Into DNA of Native Americans" OCTOBER 3RD, 2017, Updated: SEP 13, 2018, https://indiancountrytoday.com/archive/trauma-may-be-woven-into-dna-of-native-americans (August 17, 2016).

139 Jason Mandryk. *Operation World* (Colorado Springs: Biblica 2010), 866 - 867.

140 Tudor Bismark. "Bastard Curse/Spirit & Prayer~Bishop Tudor Bismark." https://www.youtube.com/watch?v=tDXR-dIb7dY (May 5, 2019)

141 Jason Mandryk, *Operation World* (Colorado Springs: Biblica 2010), 270, 719.

142 William Sears, MD., *Parenting and Childcare, a Guide for Christian Parents* (Nashville: Thomas Nelson 1993), 115, 117, 129, 150-151, 186.

143 Eloyse Ephraim Badgett, "Nebiros, Book, *Men who Hate Women* ..." CLF, October 30, 1987, 2/9.

144 Dr. Susan Forward and Joan Torres, *Men Who Hate Women and the Women Who Love Them* (New York: Bantam, 1986), 8.

145 Thomas Gregory Stewart, *The Broken Scout* (Enumclaw, WA: Redemption, 2017), 243.

146 Paul Hegstrom, *Broken Children, Grown-up Pain* (Kansas City, MO: Beacon Hill. 2001) 11.

147 Life Skills International. Lifeskillsintl.org

148 Rich Buhler, *Pain and Pretending* (Nashville: Thomas Nelson, 1988), 31.

149 Buhler, *Pain*, Ibid, 33.

150 Dr. Mohan Nair, https://mohannairmd.com/

151 PTSD, ICD-11 for Mortality and Morbidity Statistics (Version: 05/2021). https://icd.who.int/browse11/l-m/en#http%3a%2f%2fid.who.int%2ficd%2fentity%2f2070699808 (December 20, 2021).

152 CPTSD, ICD-11 for Mortality and Morbidity Statistics (Version: 05/2021) Geneva, 05/2021. https://icd.who.int/browse11/l-m/en#/http%253a%252f%252fid.who.

Endnotes

int%252ficd%252fentity%252f585833559(December 20, 2021).

153 "The Best Story," (Moundridge, Kansas: Gospel Tract and Bible Society) gtbs.org 620-345-2533

154 Jack T. Chick, "Are Roman Catholics Christians?" (Jack T. Chick LLC. 1985). 15.

155 Anna Paraseah, "Sex sins or Acting out." CLF, January 21, 2001.

156 Anna Paraseah, A-Z demon names. Luciferina. CLF.

157 Anna Paraseah, Interrogate, CLF.

158 Pastor Eloyse Badgett, "Boniface deliverance pattern." CLF. October 9, 1976.

159 Jack Chick, "Evil Eyes" (Ontario, CA: Chick, 2019). chick.org

160 Ex Satanist - John Ramirez Testimony January 22, 2019. https://www.youtube.com/watch?v=uqyAsHr8ZRY

163 Pastor Eloyse Badgett, "Deliverance and Healing for the Woman who has had an Abortion," CLF, January 8, 2004.

164 Rev. Terry Taylor. "Satan has 80 Horrifying demons that can take possession of your body." The NTL Tattler, Exorcism Special (Chicago: "Publisher's Promotion Agency, Inc." Spring 1974), 11.

165 Anna Paraseah, Beelzebub, *A-Z demon names*, CLF.

166 Eliphas Levi, *The Mysteries of Magic*, 1886. 74-75.

167 Albert Pike, *Morals and Dogma*, 1987. 734

168 Yvonne Kitchen, *Freemasonry Death in The Family* (Mountain Gate, Victoria: Fruitful Vine, 1997), 117, 142 media@fruitfulvine.org

169 Eloyse Ephraim Badgett, "Put Satanachia deliverance pattern." CLF. November 7, 1985.

170 Anna Paraseah, Summary of Many Put Satanachia Deliverance Patterns, *A-Z demon names and summary*, CLF.

171 Eloyse Ephraim Badgett, "Psychic Power and Shame Patterns," *Handbook for Strategic Level Spiritual Warfare for the Middle East and Europe* (Lakewood, CO: Lakewood Foursquare Church/Christian Living Fellowship, 1996), 4.1-5.11.

172 Anna Paraseah, *A-Z Dictionary*, Depression, CLF.

173 Anna Paraseah, Sargatanas and Zireck. *A-Z Demon Names*, CLF

174 Pastor Eloyse Badgett, *"Nebiros."* CLF. pg. 1/2.

175 Anna Paraseah, Lucifuge Roficale, *A-Z demon names.* CLF.

176 Eloyse Ephraim Badgett, *"Homosexuality Spirits,"* CLF, February 10, 1993.

177 Eloyse Ephraim Badgett, "Sexual Lust Demons." *Handbook for Strategic Level Spiritual Warfare for the Middle East and Europe* (Lakewood, CO: Lakewood Foursquare Church/Christian Living Fellowship, 1996), 6.1-6.8.

178 Eloyse Ephraim Badgett, "Put Satanachia, Perverse spirit," CLF.

179 Anna Paraseah, *A-Z Demon names.* Put S. Baal. CLF.

180 Anna Paraseah, *A-Z Demon names.* Isis. CLF.

181 Badgett, "Sexual Lust Demons." *Osiris. Strategic Level Spiritual Warfare*, 6.1.

182 Badgett, "Sexual Lust Demons." Sargatanas. *Strategic Level Spiritual Warfare*, 6.2.

183 Eloyse Ephraim Badgett, "Proxy Deliverance for a Woman," CLF. January 22, 1989.

184 Miranda Hitti, "Herpes and Oral Sex: Women's Risks," Genital Herpes News March 1, 2005, https://www.

Endnotes

webmd.com/genital-herpes/news/20050301/herpes-oral-sex-womens-risks

185 Jasmine Townsend, *It Could Have Been Me*, (Colorado Springs: Hunter Heart, 2013).

186 Pastor Eloyse Badgett, "Spirits to cast out Immediately: (All under Satan)." CLF.

187 Anna Paraseah, *A-Z Dictionary*, death spirits. CLF.

188 Lilly Hope Lucario August 17, 2017 https://themighty.com/2017/08/life-impacting-symptoms-of-complex-post-traumatic-stress-disorder-ptsd/

189 Jack T. Chick, *The Big Betrayal* (Ontario, CA: Chick, 1981). 48, 58, 59.

190 Charles Chiniquy, *Fifty Years in the Church of Rome* (Chino: Chick, 1958), 309.

191 Edmond Paris, *The Secret History of the Jesuits*, (Chino: Chick, 1983), 191.

191 Jack T. Chick, *Jesuits*, vol. 20, (Ontario, CA: Chick, 2011), 29, 30.

192 Jack T. Chick, *The Prophet*, Alberto Part 6, vol. 17, (Ontario, CA: Chick, 1988).

193 Jack T. Chick, *The Force*, Alberto Part 4, vol. 15, (Ontario, CA: Chick, 1983), 24, 25.

194 "The New World Order of Ignatius De Loyola," August 17, 2008 https://ignatiusdeloyola.blogspot.com/

195 The Editors of *Encyclopaedia Britannica*, "Aimee Semple McPherson American religious leader," https://www.britannica.com/biography/Aimee-Semple-McPherson

196 "Taking the Aspie Quiz," Asperger's Tests musings of an Aspie. November 20, 2012 https://musingsofanaspie.com/2012/11/20/taking-the-aspie-quiz/ (November 16, 2020).

197 Pastor Eloyse Badgett, Autism deliverances. CLF. July 29, 1984.

198 Pastor Eloyse Badgett, "Autism Demons and Definitions." CLF.

199 Yvonne Kitchen. *Freemasonry Death in The Family.* (Mountain Gate, Victoria: Fruitful Vine, 1997), 150-152. media@fruitfulvine.org

200 Mina R. Brawner, MD., *Woman in the Word* (Dallas: Christ for the Nations, 1975), 50-52, 54-55.

201 Eloyse Ephraim Badgett, "The Death Spirit, Apollyon/Abaddon, Ministry on our Secret Sins." Christian Living Fellowship, Lakewood, Colorado. 6-19-81.

202 Eloyse Ephraim Badgett, "Angels of Death." Christian Living Fellowship, Lakewood, Colorado. 7-23-88.

203 Eloyse Ephraim Badgett, "Merodach" deliverance pattern, Christian Living Fellowship, Lakewood, Colorado. April 1981. 2.

204 Eloyse Ephraim Badgett, The Death Spirit, Apollyon/Abaddon. CLF. June 19, 1981.

205 Anna Paraseah. *"Death Spirits." A-Z Dictionary.* CLF Eloyse Ephraim Badgett, Krodeus Deliverance Pattern. July 15,1976. 206Anna Paraseah, "Krodeus deliverance ministry, July 15, 1976." CLF.

206 Anna Paraseah, "Krodeus deliverance ministry, July 15, 1976." CLF

207 Anna Paraseah. Zeus. *A-Z Demon Names.* CLF.

208 Dr. Meri Crouley, Freedom Cry: Women Fighting Trafficking (Brigham City: New Life Clarity 2022) https://mericrouley.com

209 the people'sprayernetwork.com

210 Frédéric Saliba, "Mexico's rebel Chiapas state is turning its back on Catholicism" Apr 10, 2012 https://www.

theguardian.com/world/2012/apr/10/mexico-indians-abandon-catholic-church July 9, 2023.

211 Sun Dance religious ceremony. Arts & Culture; https://www.britannica.com/topic/Sun-Dance. (July 9, 2023).

212 Andrew Van Dam, "It ended in 1767, yet this experiment is still linked to higher incomes and education levels today." https://www.washingtonpost.com/business/2018/11/09/years-after-jesuits-were-expelled-towns-near-their-missions-still-have-higher-education-incomes/ July 9, 2023

213 Eloyse Ephraim Badgett, "Sexual Lust Demons," Handbook for Strategic Level Spiritual Warfare for the Middle East and Europe (Lakewood, CO: Lakewood Foursquare Church/Christian Living Fellowship, 1996) Pages 6.1 -6.8.

214 Wes Penre, "The Secret Order of the Illuminati, A brief History of Moriah and the Shadow Government," November 27, 2003, Last Updated: June 10, 2005 from Illuminati-News Website. https://www.bibliotecapleyades.net/sociopolitica/esp_sociopol_illuminati_12.htm

References

Contact for Authors

Rebecca Brown, MD., (1948-2020) and Daniel Yoder, Harvestwarriors.com. e-mail warriors@artelco.com

Yvonne Kitchen, Fruitful Vine, 500 Kelletts Road, Lysterfield, 3156, Melbourne, Victoria, Australia. media@fruitfulvine.org.

Irene A. Park, Pastor Herb and Sandy Pohlmeyer, Christ Deliverance Ministries Internet Church http://cdmin.com/ Pastor Pohlmeyer sells Park's book and a PDF of her seven booklets.

Selwyn Stevens, PhD., Jubilee Resources International Inc. PO Box 3, Feilding, 4740 New Zealand, Web: jubileeresources.org Arsenal Books. https://www.arsenalbooks.com/Selwyn-Stevens-s/1900.htm 888-563-5150.

Books

Thomas R. Horn & Terry James, *Antichrist and the Final Solution (Crane*, MO; Defender, 2020).

TonyaAnn Pember, Inside Story: *52 Weeks in the Word* (Littleton: Illumify Media, 2021). https://tonyaann.com/

Maurice Rawlings, MD., *To Hell and Back* (Nashville: Thomas Nelson 1993).

David H. Stern, *Jewish New Testament Commentary* (Clarksville, MD: Jewish New Testament Pub, Inc., 1989). Matt. 1:21.

References

Children

Mary Jo Pennington, *6 Big Big Big Angels* (Brandon, FL: Big Angels Press, 2005).

Elspeth Campbell Murphy, *David and I talk to God Series* (Colorado Springs: David C. Cook, Chariot).

Janie-sue Wertheim and Kathy Shapiro, *Walk with Y'shua Through the Jewish Year* (San Francisco: Purple Pomegranate, 1998).

Allie Slocum, an elementary school teacher; children's books on forgiveness, compassion, integrity, respect, and responsibility. https://www.amazon.com/Allie-Slocum/e/B07K5GHDHN/ref=dp_byline_cont_pop_ebooks_1

Jane Werner Watson, Switzer, Hirschberg, *Children's books on emotions*, "Created in Cooperation with The Menninger Foundation for Solving the Problems of Childhood."

Catholicism

Selwyn Stevens Ph.D., *Rome's Anathemas* (Wellington, N Z: Jubilee Resources, 2016). A ten-page renouncing prayer for Catholicism.

Use the Deliverance List for Familiar Spirits, Appendix G, to cast out the spirits of Ignatius of Loyola, the founder of the Illuminati and the Jesuits.

Parenting

Dr. Sears, "*Ask Dr. Sears.*" https://www.askdrsears.com/topics/parenting/attachment-parenting/unconnected-child (August 21, 2020). Dr. Wm. Sears, himself and several sons.

Messianic

Ron Cantor, "I am looking for the FOURTH Temple!" Sep 29, 2022https://www.roncantor.com/post/i-am-looking-for-the-fourth-temple

Freemasonry

Selwyn Stevens Ph.D., *Unmasking Freemasonry Removing the Hoodwink* (Wellington, N Z: Jubilee Resources, 2007).

The renouncing prayer for freemasonry is on Selwyn Steven's website, identical to the prayer in his book, beginning on page 48. https://jubileeresources.org/pages/freemasonry (May 18, 2022).

SMART – Stop Mind Control and Ritual Abuse Today. https://ritualabuse.us/

Mormonism

Utah Lighthouse Ministry. http://www.utlm.org/

Selwyn Stevens Ph.D., Unmasking Mormonism (Wellington, N Z: Jubilee Resources, 2007).

Use The Deliverance List for Familiar Spirits, Appendix G, to cast out the spirits of the founder, Joseph Smith, who was a Freemason.

Teens and Women

Lisa Bevere, Purity's Power DVD video sessions (Colorado Springs: Messenger International 2004).

Loren Cunningham, David Joel Hamilton, Why Not Women? (Seattle: YWAM, 2000).

Dr. Margaret J. Rinck, Christian Men who Hate Women (Grand Rapids: Zondervan 1990)

Safer Resource, "The Evidence is in: inequality, fixed gender roles and patriarchal teachings can help create church environments where abuse of women can thrive." Faith Women, Inequality and the Church, Australia. https://www.saferresource.org.au/women_inequality_and_the_church (May 7, 2020).

Marilyn VanDerbur, "Once Can Hurt a Lifetime." 2018. This video addresses sexually inappropriate behavior

References

between children and teens. https://www.youtube.com/watch?v=8h19yf45vwo

Deliverance and Healing; Books and Literature

Micah Stephen Bell, Breaking Free (Euless, TX: Key Ministries, 2009). https://www.keydeliverance.org/copy-of-videos-1, https://www.keyministries.org/

Jack Chick's tracts available to read online in many subjects and languages. Chick.com

Patricia Baird Clark, Restoring Survivors of Ritual Abuse, (His Presence Publishers, Atlanta, NY 14808, 2010, 2017). 33. https://hispresenceonline.org/

Rebecca Brown and Daniel Yoder, Unbroken Curses: *Hidden Source of Trouble in the Christian's Life* (New Kensington: Whitaker House 1995).

Jonas Clark, *Rejection is Hell* (Hallandale, FL: Spirit of Life, 2002). I used this book in the Bible study for the mentally ill.

Gene Moody: 12 deliverance Manuals in pdf format. www.genemoody.com/manuals.html

Jess Parker, *The Myth of Multiple Personality Disorder?* (Yuba City: TDS Ministries).

Derek Prince, *Blessing or Curse: You Can Choose* (Grand Rapids: Chosen, 1990).

Michael Reagan, *Twice Adopted* (Nashville. Broadman & Holman. 2004).

Merrill, F. Unger, *What Demons Can Do to Saints*, (Chicago: Moody, New edition 1991).

Merrill, F. Unger, *Biblical Demonology: A Study of Spiritual Forces at Work Today*, (Wheaton: Van Kampen, 2011).

Gary Whetstone, *How to Identify and Remove Curses* (New Castle, DE: Gary Whetstone. 1998).

Know You Have Eternal Life

Deliverance and Healing Ministries

Don't go alone to counsel with a person of the opposite sex. Stay in the session with a child.

Beit Tikvah Foursquare Messianic Congregation, Newcastle, WA 98059.http://beittikvah.us

David and Cheryl Bryan, Church of Glad Tidings, Live Oak, CA 95953, Isaiah 61 Deliverance Conferences, online. https://churchofgladtidings.com/ info@churchofgladtidings.com 530-671-3160

Cornerstone Television Network info@ctvn.org 24/7 Prayer Line: 888-665-4483

Life Skills International.Paul Hegstrom 1941-2017.info@lifeskillsintl.org. 806-348-7171.

Lake Hamilton Bible Camp, Arkansas.https://lakehamiltonbiblecamp.com. 501-525-8204.

Mark Hemans, "Jesus Encounter Ministries." Live meetings and ONLINE meetings in English with Spanish and other translators. At the end of every four-hour meeting everyone receives ministry in a group. Check his schedule frequently and register for Live or ONLINE meetings. Only a donation is requested. https://www.youtube.com/channel/UCmMLO7vxbA78hTr6EgguIYA https://www.jesusencounterministries.com. Also see YouTubes.

YouTubes

See Hemans, above.

Carlos Oliveira. "4 HOURS Brother Carlos Casting Out Your Demons." https://www.youtube.com/watch?v=PF6RrWD4nbs

Evangelist Fernando Perez. "1 Hour of Powerful Spiritual Warfare Prayer Against Curses and Demons." https://www.youtube.com/watch?v=AnY9qakBYBA

Ex Satanist - John Ramirez Testimony January 22, 2019. https://www.youtube.com/watch?v=uqyAsHr8ZRY

Scouting

Use The Deliverance List for Familiar Spirits, Appendix G, to cast out the spirits of the founders. Robert Baden-Powell, the Wolf Cub and Boy Scouts, a Freemason. Boyle and Gunn say that he had the characteristics of a Pedophile. Dr. E. Urner Goodman and Carroll Edson, the Boy Scout Order of the Arrow, Freemasons. Juliette Gordon Low, the Girl Scouts.

Patrick Boyle and Robert Gunn, *Scout's Honor, Sexual Abuse in America's most trusted institution* (Kindle edition, Amazon, 2013) https://www.amazon.com/Scouts-Honor-Patrick-Boyle/dp/1559583657 (February 19, 2020).

Boy Scouts of America, *Order of the Arrow Handbook* (Irving, TX Boy Scouts of America. 1991).

Jack Burns, "Boy Scouts Pay Out Nearly a Billion for 60,000 Sex Abuse Victims and Almost No Arrests Were Made," Child Health, Crime, July 6, 2021. https://www.activistpost.com/2021/07/boy-scouts-pay-out-nearly-a-billion-for-60000-sex-abuse-victims-and-almost-no-arrests-were-made.html (October 3, 2022).

Thomas Gregory Stewart, *The Broken Scout.* (Enumclaw, WA: Redemption, 2017).

Lauren del Valle, "Judge grants final approval of Boy Scouts of America reorganization plan to pay more than $2.4 billion in sex abuse claims." September 9, 2022, CNN, https://www.cnn.com/2022/09/09/us/boy-scouts-of-america-bankruptcy-judge-final-approval/index.html (October 3, 2022).

Life Issues

National Right to Life, https://www.nrlc.org/medethics/willtolive/states/ (September 29, 2022).

Persecution

Alliance Defending Freedom. World-Wide Legal assistance. https://adflegal.org/

Jack T. Chick, The Crusaders, Alberto Rivera's story, parts one to six, (Chino: Chick Publications).

Corrie Ten Boom House. https://www.corrietenboom.com/en/home (October 4, 2022).

Nora Lam, China Cry (Green Forest, AR: New Leaf Press, 1984).

Richard Wurmbrand, If That Were Christ Would You Give Him your Blanket? (Waco: Word, 1970).

Wurmbrand referenced: Lavrentii Beria, Brain-Washing: A Synthesis of the Russian Text Book on Psychopolitics (Revised Edition with Foreword Added) 1959. Charles Stickley & L. Ron Hubbard. Contributors.

Addendum I

Inter tribal Wars in Africa

In chapter three of Dr. Rebecca Brown's book, Unbroken Curses, Brown speaks of the inherited sins of the forefathers which are affecting the Afro-Americans and recent African refugees. She discerns that the intertribal wars in Africa have become gang warfare in the United States of America.

Brown reminds us that in Nehemiah 9:1-3, the people confessed the sins of their fathers. In Daniel 9:11, he is remitting the sins of disobedience to God by his people who were soon to be released from Babylon, admitting that this had brought a curse.

I spoke of the Witchcraft from Africa in My Story chapter regarding My Father's Induction into the Boy Scout Order of the Arrow, and also regarding church music in: Have No Other Gods chapter. I spoke of the need to deliver out the traumas in your genetic code in the Deliverance from Traumas chapter. (See Appendix E, Fleurety, the 80-list)

Addendum II

Chapter 5. Know You Have Eternal Life and Questionnaire

The Answer to my Four Questions in Four Hispanic churches and one Other Church

Two of the Hispanic churches where people responded did so after a Passover teaching, repenting of their sins, accepting the body and blood of Yeshua, and taking the bread and cup. The other, after repenting and accepting Yeshua's blood to wash away their sins.

Ten of the twelve persons who were not sure of going to heaven knew that Jesus died for their sins. This contradicts the belief that people who are not sure of going to heaven have rejected the Savior.

There is a mistaken belief that if one is a Christian or if he has the Holy Spirit, he will not need deliverance. The Holy Spirit, on the other hand, exposes what a person needs deliverance from. Deliverance ministries could not operate without the Holy Spirit. In Mark 16:17, one sign of a believer is listed as deliverance. Many Christians are receiving deliverance now.

Four of the twelve who were not sure of going to heaven said they were going to heaven because of God instead of Jesucristo?

In a Hispanic Evangelical Charismatic Church after a Passover teaching, March 2021

Some had left after the service. Of those who stayed, eight were sure, eight were not sure of going to heaven. One would not, another could not respond.

In a Hispanic Charismatic Church after a Passover teaching, April 2023

Approximately six people did not answer the questions.

Of those who did, four were sure, four were not sure of going to heaven.

In a Hispanic Church, May 2023

Five were sure, fifteen were not sure of going to Heaven.

In a Hispanic Messianic Congregation December 2022 and January 2023

Although I had left this congregation years ago, I was warmly received. I love these people.

No one was sure of going to heaven, except a young man who repented of his sins using the Ten Commandments.

This congregation clings to the false doctrine of "soul sleep," believing that one rests in the grave after death to await the judgment. Apostle Paul said when we are absent from the body, he will be present with the Lord. (2 Cor. 5:8).

In a Church of Recent African Refugees

The assistant pastor, also the musical leader, responded, "that's a private matter," when I told him I wanted him to be sure of going to heaven.

One person believes that he is going to hell. One influential believing member said he is going to heaven, "because God told me I would."

Teenagers or young adults from at least 3 families are not sure of going to heaven, even though their parents are.

I dedicated my book to a woman from South America who attended this church one time.

Three of these five churches belong to denominations. Independent churches are best, but they can be infiltrated, like the others, by witches, Freemasons or Jesuits. (See Appendix I).

This entire book is written for people inside or outside the church who don't know they have eternal life, But especially for the Hispanic people.

The curses of the Inquisition must be cast out. In Have No Other Gods chapter, I teach that church festivals, and sometimes church music are filled with witchcraft. I explain the bondages that come from infant baptism, catechism, the worship of Mary, the Jesuits and their symbol, the I H S, from Freemasonry and Scouting. I explain the need to cast out the mixing of ancestry with the indigenous peoples, as with any race that practiced witchcraft, due to sacrifices of children that are being made to the god, Molech. Some Hispanics have married or become Muslims. Deliverance from curses and trauma is addressed in these specific chapters. The Appendices contain valuable deliverance lists.

Chapter 9. Teaching on Actual Deliverance

Spiritual Warfare

Dr. Brown, in chapter 16 of Prepare For War, opposes the vegetarian diet advocated by New Age religions. In times of intense spiritual warfare, she eats meat at least twice a day. She says that without protein you can become weak, sick and unable to fight off infections. I quote Providence in COVID-19 deliverance on my website, givingyeshua.com. I learned that I had to eat 75-100 mg. of protein a day when recovering from COVID-19.

While prayer walking along with spiritual warfare, I have walked around churches, medical facilities, homes and housing units. In a multi-dwelling unit where drugs were allegedly sold, more and more information was obtained about the problem each time. I sympathized with the cries of both the residents and the homeless who were being victimized. I shared this information with the police and the HOA board. The drug traffickers were evicted, arrested or moved. Then, Yeshua told me to pray for the homeless people who still came to a unit, so I asked Yeshua to forgive their sins. (See Remitting Sins chapter). Although one woman was stabbed, she was not killed, but was later evicted. These victories came at the cost of being vilified by other residents because of my testimony and my care for these people. But a man came back to say that he was saved in prison and had a job. Another thanked me for paying for his bus ticket to a homeless shelter on a freezing day. And I ministered to a dear woman on a rainy day.

Chapter 10 Deliverance from Curses

A Tithe Broke the Spell (Malachi 3:8-12).

After a wedding, some members of our family began having surgeries due to injuries, and my husband and I lost four checks in the mail. My husband began tithing and the spell on our money was broken. In addition, when I used the list in Appendix G, Yeshua showed me who sent the spell over my family at the wedding. I have tithed since my first husband left us. My second husband and I gave $100 as seed faith to Pastor Rodney Howard Brown in 1996 to get a house. We were blessed with 3 grants and a small mortgage to purchase our small condo.

Chapter 10 Deliverance from Curses

Krodeus, the Bastard Curse

Deliver this curse, Krodeus, along with other known curses, out of persons who are not sure of going to heaven. I am now chosen, adopted and accepted in the Beloved. (Eph. 1:4-6). I have been grafted into the body of believers. (Rom. 9:26; 11:17). Deliverances by Anna in 1999 gave me freedom. Although my mom and dad were married when I was conceived, this spirit came in because I took on the spirit of a child who was conceived out of wedlock. I also had the bondages below that make Krodeus enter.

Adopted people often have this spirit. The conception may have been in rape. The baby may have been aborted or another means of birth control may have been used. Cast out the spirit of Molech along with Krodeus.

Pastor Eloyse learned that this master curse, the bastard curse, is called Krodeus. CLF patterns indicate that this curse works to destroy the body, soul and spirit. This spirit also comes in as the namesake of a cursed person, infant baptism and all sexual sins and sexual traumas. It also enters with scouting, freemasonry, witchcraft, and is inherited. Krodeus brings diseases in the kidneys, gastrointestinal tract, upper respiratory system and severe pain throughout the body.

Before receiving deliverance, there is guilt, with denial of the bondage and fear of not being saved. There is fear, victimization, desire to sleep, feelings of rejection and addictions, especially to sin. Krodeus can enter secretly, by watching sex and violence in the media.

Put Satanachia enters with Krodeus and also with Luciferina. (Put Satanachia, See #4, Appendix E). As Tudor Bismark teaches, this curse is the most important thing to cast out.

The Millers and Moody's, who founded Lake Hamilton Bible Camp, compiled "The Curse of the Bastard." "Lust enters and the demons of lust will follow all the children of this line." "Current observations include more bastards, family and personal rebellion, illness, suicide, inability to feel welcome or at peace in the house of God, murder, crime, and mental illness." They document dependence on the government.

Addendum II

These people may have disabilities, may be confined to a nursing home, incarcerated, or homeless.

King David conceived a bastard son by Bathsheba. (2 Sam. 11:1-5). Solomon, their second son, was plagued by lust and idolatry. He built a Moloch idol to sacrifice babies on a hill near Jerusalem. (1 Kings 11:1-8).

My teaching on Krodeus is found in several parts of this book.

(See Valentine's Day and Fornication, and Goddesses Enter with Infant Baptism, Chapter, Having No Other Gods)

(See Bismark, Traumas of Afro-Americans. Deliverance from Trauma chapter)

(See Deliverance from Abortion, Appendix D and Appendices F and N)

(See Curses Bring Addiction, Deliverances as I Witness chapter).

Addendum III

Sex Trafficking

After watching the movie Sound of Freedom, I asked, "Are Hispanic children trafficked more often?"

I found, "Child sex trafficking is a cycle of abuse," at thorn.org. Those who are most vulnerable to this type of exploitation are children: those who are homeless or runaways, LGBTQ, African American or Latino, and youth who interact with the child welfare system.

One indication that a teen or adult has been sexualized is their immodest dress. I dressed immodestly, and I see teens and women, even in church, do the same.

Crouley, in chapter 2 of Freedom Cry, reports that Mark learned in prison it is easier to sell girls than drugs. Girls attach to the pimp in a sympathetic bond called the Stockholm Syndrome. In Deliverance from Traumas chapter, I quote Herman who speaks of this as idolatry of one's abuser. This is what has been also done for pedophiles in our families and communities. The rapist sets it up so he will be able to revictimize without being suspected and reported. The victim represses the trauma or keeps it a secret, blaming and hating herself. Regarding the principalities of the 80-list, Pastor Eloyse said repression brings in #4, Put Satanachia (Baphomet) who blocks the will and the intellect and everything becomes a distortion.

Deliver rescued and recovering girls and women from the familiar spirits of their abusers, Appendix G. (See 80-list App. E., See Crouley, App. M).

Weep for Yourselves and for Your Children

Yeshua knew what the religious leaders had done and would do to women and children. (John 8:3-11). He said, "Daughters of Jerusalem, weep not for me, but weep for yourselves, and for your children." (Luke 23:28).

In the story of the woman caught in the act of adultery, only the woman was brought. Yeshua set her free saying, "He who is without sin among you, let him throw a stone at her first." (John 8:7b. See Lev. 20:10).

Attorneys love these cases. Schoener, an expert witness cases of betrayal, is quoted in the Therapy Exploitation Link Line, "Sexual Misconduct by Professionals," saying women are blamed instead of seen as victims.

An Afro-American woman was traumatized when she was 16. One night when she couldn't get into her house because her mother had locked the door, the teenage neighbor boy raped her. Her church had her confess the sin of having a baby out of wedlock. The teenage boy had joined the military. He was returned for court, but lied and went free. (Matt. 18:6)

Extreme damage is done by rape, by victimization by a person in a position of authority, and by religious abuse, no matter at what age. (See Beck, The Defilement of Women, Deliverance from Traumas chapter).

I kept repeating my trauma. A woman counselor at a mental health center in 1982 asked me if he didn't really want my husband, instead of me! A speaker at Camp Farthest Out in 1982, yelled out what I had just told him. In 1983, an adult Sunday school teacher from the second Yokefellow group said if I didn't forgive, I would be delivered to the tormentors. These leaders were in denial, protecting themselves and their associates.

I returned to CLF in 1998, but Pastor Eloyse and Anna didn't understand these betrayals. A former Methodist pastor whom Eloyse had appointed over counseling had an adulterous relationship with a young woman, and in 1978 took most of her members.

I had made bad choices that were forced on me by being blackmailed and seduced by the Yokefellow group leader. He had victimized our whole family, in the end, by the divorce and lingering trauma. (Gen. 12:1-20, 20:1-17).

Finally, I found fairness. In 1990 Dr. S. told me the Yokefellow group leader knew he should not be sexually involved with a person he was counseling because of the harm it causes. Yeshua heals the brokenhearted and sets the captives free, (Luke 4:18, 8:1-3)

Violence Against Messianic Jews

Some ultra-Orthodox Jews in Israel have taken part in "Violent Protest Against Messianic Jews in Jerusalem." RonCantor.com/media. Ron Cantor's wife was attacked before she could enter a prayer meeting. (See the book of Acts in the Bible for these same persecutions).

Antichrist Spirits and the Illuminati

The information that we will have another covid lockdown has caused me to prepare this brief addendum for you to use in spiritual warfare.

Pastor Eloyse listed five master spirits of the Antichrist. Python, deception. Zeus, idolatry. Hercules, false redemption. Bacchus, false eternal life (alcoholism). Apollo, false salvation, the intellect. Python, See Symbols and Emblems that Bring Curses chapter.

There are many Antichrists. (1 John 2:18). The spirit of Molech. The Anti-Semitic spirit of Luther. Marion (Mary, Isis) and Boniface. (Ap. B). The spirit of Jezebel, rejection of one's father, and autism. July 8, 1977.

Pastor Eloyse discerned spirits over the Illuminati (Moriah Conquering Wind): Pan, Priapus, Remphan (Acts 7:43), Baal-Peor (Num. 25:1-3), and Janus, ruling by brainwashing and humanism.

Penre states "the goals of the Illuminati ... are to create a One World Government and a New World Order, with them on top to rule the world into slavery and fascism." They have especially targeted the youth through movies, fine arts and music that leads them into "robotism", apathy, violence, drugs and brings control of their minds.

He lists 13 families of the Illuminati: Astor, Bundy, Collins, DuPont, Freeman, Kennedy, Li (Chinese), Onassis, Rockefeller, Rothschild, Russell, van Duyn, Merovingian (European Royal Families). Interconnected are Reynolds, Disney, Krupp, McDonald and hundreds of others, more distant.214

Evicted from all Mental Health Center Groups

The Courage to Heal book by Bass and Davis, was given to me in a trauma support group in 1990. I found a footnote that warned about abuse under hypnosis, which helped me regain my memories about Dr. M. 26 years later I revealed this in a trauma support group, also saying I discarded the book because the authors were lesbian. Then I received a call that I could never participate in groups at that mental health center.

Homosexuality, lesbianism, and transsexuality are prevalent among survivors of sexual abuse.

Read in Appendix F. of my miracle deliverance in 2020. Two pastors are glad to see these deliverances, because they counsel many couples who have problems.

INDEX

Appendices and Addendums

Appendices

- A Deliverance from Infant Baptism and the Order of the Arrow. 111
- B Boniface Deliverance Pattern. 113
- C More Deliverances for the Sephardic Jews, other Jews and Believers 118
- D Deliverance from Abortion, Birth Control, and other Unbiblical Practices 119
- E The 80-List, Eight Principalities 122
- F Miracle Homosexual Deliverance 128
- G The Deliverance List for Familiar Spirits 131
- H Complex PTSD, Lucario 134
- I More on the Jesuits 135
- J Not Being Able to Speak Up 137
- K Spirits Over Death 139
- L American Indian Deliverances 141
- M Deliverance from Spirits of Indigenous Peoples 143
- N Sexual Lust Demons 146
- O Postpartum Depression 151

Addendum I

Intertribal Wars in Africa 178

Addendum II

Appendices

    Chapter 5. The Answer to my Four Questions 179
    Chapter 9. Spiritual Warfare 181
    Chapter 10. The Tithe Broke the Spell 182
    Chapter 10. Krodeus, the Bastard Curse 182

Addendum III
    Sex Trafficking 185
    Weep for Yourselves and for Your Children 186
    Violence Against Messianic Jews 187
    Anti-Christ Spirits and the Illuminati 187
    Evicted from all Mental Health Center Groups 188

INDEX

BOOK

A

Abortion. 51, 53, 54, 75, 86, 96, 98, 103, App. D, 119, 120.

Abuse. 4, 9, 17, 23, 51, 53, 54, 56, 57, 63, 65, 68, 71, 75, 76, 80, Ch. 11, 98, 102, 103, 111, 112, 123, 125, 128-130, 133, 137, 147, 149, 173, 174, 176, 185, 186.

Africa, African. 21, 28, 65, 89, 90, 124, 143, 178, 180, 185.

Antichrist, Anti-messiah. 7, 10, 62, 69, 83, 130, 144, 171, 187, 188.

B

Biblical Feasts. Chapters 6, 9, 27, 29, 50, 69, 82, 121.

Baphomet 81, 111, 123, 130, 185.

BAPTISM, immersion, 21, 54, 55, 75, 101.

Mormon 96, 140

Infant, Sprinkling 4, 21, 23-25, 28 - 32, 37, 38, 40, 50, 51, 55 - 58, 79, 93, 96, 97, 99, 101, 102, 114, 102, 137, 139, 140, 181, 183.

Deliverance from, Appendix A., 111, 112.

Bastard. 7, 51, 62, 81, 89, 130, 182 - 184.

Betrayal. 22, 132, 186, 187.

Beelzebub. 11, 19, 23, 68, 73, 74, 81, 82, 111, 112, 122, 123, 128, 137, 140.

Buddhism, Buddha. 54, 97, 69.

C

Cabala, Kabbala, Kabbalah, Kabbalat. 47, 61, 69

Cancer. 26, 80, 123, 131, 142, 149

CATHOLOCISM. 4, 8, 10, 16, 18, 25, 28 – 30, 52, 55, 59 – 62, 65, 82, 86 – 89, 95, 96, 118, 135, 136, 144, 146, 172

Deliverance from, App. B. 112 – 117

A Catholic woman, true salvation. 129

Childhood Traumas. 19, 90

Christmas. 18, 50, 51, 54

CHURCHES

Assembly of God. 20, 22, 88

False. 135

Foursquare. 74, 136, 138, 175

Lutheran. 5, 18, 22, 31, 50, 58, 60, 80, 82, 87, 88, 90

Messianic. 2, 5, 31, 38, 43, 45 – 47 68, 69, 89, 172, 175, 180, 187

Methodist. 187

Mormon. See baptism. 61, 135, 173

Four Hispanic churches. 37, 38, 179

COVID-19, isolation, Zombie. 6, 71, 80, 81, 118, 152, 181, 187

CURSES, Chapters 8, 10. 17 – 21, 24, 25, 27, 29, 30, 36, 37, 40, 46, 51, 54 – 57, 60 – 65, 72, 74, 76, 77 – 84, 89, 90, 92, 96, 101 – 103, 108, 111, 118, 119, 123, 124, 128 – 132, 137, 140, 142, 175 – 176, 178, 181 – 184, 188

How Enter. 77.

Difference between spells and curses. 78

What curses do to you. 78

How to remove curses. 81

Antisemitic curse. 82, 83

On Firstborn. 83

From Freemasonry. 160 – 162

D

DEATH, 9, 19, 32, 33, 43 – 45, 50, 54, 57, 58, 61, 65, 68, 78 – 81, 83, 84, 86, 89, 92, 99, 107, 109, 111, 112, 115, 118 – 121, 133, 136, App, K, 139 – 140, 145, 147, 149, 152, 153, 163, 180

Death wish that attacks the brain, 19, 78, 140

Death, spiritual, 38, 57, 140

Deliverance, Instructions, pg. 11. Chapters 9, 10, 11, 13. Appendices, 111 – 153. Addendums.

DEPRESSION. 19, 61, 88, 93, 94, 124, 130

Bipolar. 124

Postpartum, 19, App. O. pgs. 151 – 153

Divorce. 19, 53, 80, 81, 83, 92, 187

Drums. 21, 52, 65, 141

Druid. 18, 61, 119

E

Easter. 41, 43, 50 – 52, 84

Egyptian god Osiris. 51, 54, 56, 57, 60, 61, 111, 124, 128, 130, 140, 147

Egyptian goddess Isis. 16, 22, 56, 59 – 61, 101, 124, 128, 130, 137, 140, 147, 188

Epigenetics. 89, 118

F

Familiar Spirit. See Zombie. App. G. 18, 22, 51, 59, 61, 64, 75, 76, 81, 83, 89, 103, 104, 120, 131, 172, 173, 176, 186.

Fear, fearful, fearing. App. G. pgs. 131 – 133. See Zombie. 13, 18, 19, 22, 33, 54, 57, 78, 85, 99, 105, 109, 111, 120, 123, 125, 130

G

Guide spirit. 112, 123, 144

H

Hispanic. 5, 8, 25, Chapter 3; 28 – 30, 38, 65, 68, 89, 179 – 181, 185.

Hindu, Hinduism. 26, 61, 62, 86, 97, 121, 123, 130, 135.

Holy Spirit; counterfeit, false. 106, 123

Holy Spirit, Pentecost. 45

Homosexual. 128 – 130, 140, 142, 147

I

Illuminati. 7, 135, 136, 172, 187, 188

Indian, American, Indigenous tribes, Appendices L & M, pgs. 141 – 146. 21, 28, 51, 63 – 65, 67, 89, 130, 181

Inquisition. Chapter 3; pgs. 27 – 30. 8, 63, 88, 89, 118, 135, 181

J

Jesuit. Appendix I. Pgs. 135 – 136. 16, 29, 59, 60, 68, 146, 172, 181

K

KRODEUS. Master curse. 7, 81, 90, 103, 123, 157, 169, 182 – 184.

And addictions. 103.

From fornication. 51.

And homosexuality. 129 – 130.

From infant baptism. 51, 56, 101, 140.

From sexual abuse and sex sins. 129, 130.

From sexual betrayal. 22

L

Luther. 18, 24, 56, 78, 81, 83, 84, 92, 113, 188

M

Mikvah. 47

Molech. 51, 53 – 55, 64, 65, 68, 102, 120, 130, 139, 142, 181, 183, 188

N

New Testament, burning of. 61

New Testament, names of demons in. 73, 74

P

Passover. 43, 46, 47, 83, 84, 179, 180

Python, Pythoness. 68, 84, 108, 123, 128 – 131, 133, 147, 188

S

Sabbath. Chapter 6; pgs. 41-47. 4, 5, 9 – 11, 22, 24, 27

Satanic ritual abuse and days. 52 – 54, 65, 68, 86, 130

Scouts, Cub, Boy, Girl. Appendix A. pgs. 111, 112. 9, 21, 40, 56, 61, 64, 65, 67, 75, 80, 90, 93, 99, 130, 137, 141, 176, 178, 181, 183

SEPARATION, Isolation. 63, 81, 92, 152

And Solomon's sins. 27, 44, 69, 184

Sephardic Jews. Chapter 3; 27 – 30. Appendix 3; 118. 138

Sex Trafficking. Addendum 3; 185-186. 92, 152

Sin, defend it. 37, 108

Six-pointed star. Chapter 8; 67 – 69. 11, 46, 118, 129, 131, 140

Spiritual warfare. Addendum II; pg. 181, 182. 7, 9, 11, 17, 30, 31, 46, 49, 52, 73, 81, 107 – 109, 122, 128, 136, 146, 176, 187

Sun God. 51, 60, 62, 111

Symbols. Chapter 8; pgs. 67 – 69. 12, 46, 50, 56, 62, 65, 128, 129, 131, 140, 142, 148, 171, 176, 178, 181

T

Tithe, tithing, 98, 78, 182

TRAUMAS. Chapter 11, pgs. 85 – 94. 7, 9, 12, 19, 19, 20, 23, 29, 30, 40, 56, 61, 63, 72, 76, 79 – 81, 83, 185 – 187

Trauma, inherited. 89, 103, 118

Typhon. 25, 84, 111

W

War, warrior, wars. 17, 18, 25, 28, 46, 51, 59, 63, 64, 78, 86, 89, 90, 92, 124, 125, 127, 135, 140 – 142, 146, 163

Witness. 8, 9, 10, 15, 24 – 26, 39, 58, 69, 85, 99, 101, 108, 143, 184

Women in Ministry. 138

Z

Zombie. 57, 58, 81, 125, 140, 153.

www.ingramcontent.com/pod-product-compliance
Lightning Source LLC
Chambersburg PA
CBHW071202160426
43196CB00011B/2161